LONESOME *for* BEARS

A Woman's Journey in the Tracks of the Wilderness

LINDA JO HUNTER

Photographs by Amy Shapira

THE LYONS PRESS
Guilford, Connecticut
An imprint of The Globe Pequot Press

Dedicated to the memories of

Swimmer, Blondie, and Amy,

all young, trusting bears

that swam out to the wrong boat.

Author's Note

To the best of my ability and memory, the stories and observations herein are true. However, if you were a guest at Redoubt Bay Lodge, you may remember some of the incidents differently. I have consolidated some frequently occurring events into one episode. For instance, James took apart beaver lodges on a regular basis for a month and a half, so rather than describe each instance, I consolidated his behavior into one story. Likewise, guests often asked the same question or had the same reaction to things, and some of these incidents run together in the book for the same reason. Please excuse any errors or omissions, all of which are mine. I felt it wasn't appropriate to mention individual guests, but you all were part of the wonderful experience of working at Redoubt Bay and I thank you all. Photographer Amy Shapira and I hope you will join us in supporting Vital Ground, a nonprofit organization dedicated to the preservation of bear habitat and the coexistence of bears and humans. Visit them on the Internet at www.vitalground.org.

Linda Jo Hunter
Summer 2007

Contents

Author's Note iv

Preface vii

Acknowledgments ix

Chapter One: Getting Interested in Bears 1

Chapter Two: Tracking Bears 5

Chapter Three: Summer 2002 27

Chapter Four: A Bear's World 51

Chapter Five: Summer 2003 61

Chapter Six: Summer 2004 79

Chapter Seven: Summer 2005 105

Chapter Eight: Bears from Other Places 127

Suggested Further Reading 131

About the Author and Photographer 134

Preface

I grew up terrified of bears.

In 1967 I was in college when two girls were killed in Glacier National Park on the same night, pulled from their sleeping bags and eaten by bears. This was particularly frightening to me because they were both my age and doing something that I would do. The horror of this carried well into my life.

The first books I read on bears were accounts of bear attacks—stories read in my tent at night by flashlight with blood pouring off the pages. Descriptions of scalp-ripping, flesh-shredding carnage followed me into sleep. My first time in Alaska, in 1986, I was too afraid to walk anywhere by myself. I looked for bears everywhere. I was sure that one was going to run out of the woods and tear my face off. All of my early bear observations were over the shoulder of someone who was carrying a gun.

It was a long journey from being terrified of bears to missing their company. In fact it took me about fourteen years of study. When my husband, Mike McHugh, and I moved to Washington State in 1987, I discovered how much I love solo wilderness travel. I was determined to get over my fears, so I studied the art and science of tracking. Tracking has taken me down many roads. I have tracked humans for search and rescue, and taken classes from master trackers in all disciplines. Through tracking I began to learn more about animal behavior, especially the habits of the animals that frightened me the most.

I met photographer Amy Shapira for the first time at Redoubt Bay Lodge, Alaska, in the summer of 2002, during my first season there as the head guide at the lodge. It didn't take me long to realize that Amy felt the same way about bears that I do—that they are wonderful, intelligent, and interesting animals. Together we spent hours observing them and soon we saw them in new, illuminating ways. What we noticed is that just like people, bears are individuals. Certainly, Amy Shapira's special collection of photographs captures the bears' distinct personalities while relaxing, playing, eating, sleeping, and relating to each other.

I am still learning, of course, but the main thing I have discovered so far is that animals don't read the books written about them. Therefore, animals do things they are not "supposed" to do and thrive in places where they aren't supposed to exist at all.

About Redoubt Bay Lodge and Wolverine Cove

Redoubt Bay Lodge is located about eighty air miles southwest of Anchorage, just outside Lake Clark National Park, in an area also called Big River Lakes. It is a system of six lakes, connected to Cook Inlet by Big River. Big River also has north and south forks, flowing down from the surrounding mountains and glaciers. The area has two main salmon runs, sockeye in June and silver salmon in August. From Redoubt Bay Lodge, visitors board small boats to view bears feeding on salmon. The lodge entertains both overnight and day guests, with some folks flying in for just a few hours for bear viewing. The best viewing is when there are the most salmon and fishermen in Wolverine Cove. This particular viewing spot makes it possible for people to watch the same group of bears for the duration of their visits and gain a sense of a bear community.

Most of the guests enjoy great experiences with the resident bears. Some guests have said it is like watching a soap opera. *Travel & Leisure* magazine named Redoubt Bay Lodge one of the "50 Great American Adventures" in April 2005. The owners, Carl and Kirsten Dixon, entrusted the management of this very special lodge to my husband, Mike McHugh, and me for four summer seasons. We appreciate them as our employers and as responsible lodge owners. We share their concern for the environment and bears, as well as their desire to share this special place with others.

Acknowledgments

This whole project wouldn't exist if it weren't for Carl and Kirsten Dixon, and I can't thank Mike McHugh enough for giving up summers of kiteboarding to work in Alaska. I want to thank all the guides and staff who worked with Mike and me during the four seasons, and the guests who had the patience to wait for the next episode in the bear soap opera.

My friends who helped me during the writing include my sister Lianne Downey, Alan and Genie Herzog, Judy Hart and Jim Petrovic, Cat Betts, Venka Payne, and Roberta and Clint Crist. I would like to acknowledge Norma Stevens, my mother, who made me believe I could write, and Meredith Hays, who was the most help of all: Her talent for making books grow from raw material was invaluable.

Thank you to Doug Hill of Fish and Game who knew the bears well. I would also like to acknowledge the staff of the Within the Wild Alaskan Adventure Company, Redoubt Bay Lodge, from 2002 to 2005: Carl Dixon, owner; Kirsten Dixon, owner; Carly Dixon; Amanda Dixon; Jim Schmidt, expeditor; Juan Carlos Arregui; Lindsey Umlauf; Pete and Christina Norris; Brian Henry; Adam Hanson; Marty Maines; Marcy Lake; Mike Matheny; Joanna Hale; Susan James; Chad Fisher; Andrew Callahan; Brent Muller; "Spanky"; Jessica Comfort; Jeff Gartzke; Shirlena Montanye; Steve Stringham; Rocky Curnutt; Doug Jewel; Drew Hamilton; Melissa Gehring; Jeremy Bishop; Frank Massaro; Matt Habenicht; and Venka Payne

And thanks to the staff from Riversong Lodge and Winterlake Lodge who rotated through to help us with busy periods.

Chapter One

Getting Interested in Bears

The bear exploded out of the woods right next to me, his back paws landing ahead of his front ones as he covered the span of the road and then flew (getting big air) over the far edge, mowing down little trees. I was all alone and, I admit, very scared.

It was early spring in 1993, and I had decided it was safe for me to mountain bike on my own in the Gifford Pinchot National Forest, Washington. Of course this was after countless people told me that it was not safe for a woman to go by herself into any forest. After all, they said, I could get attacked by a bear, break a leg, get hopelessly lost, or even *die* out there. But, as a woman boat captain, I had already done lots of things "they" told me I couldn't do. I always figured I just needed to learn a few more new things and I would be fine.

This bear frightened me so badly that I started talking to myself. I had been eating an apple, looking at my map, and checking my route back down to the valley floor. When I stood up to get back on my bike I made some little noise; perhaps my jacket zipper hit the bike frame as I moved. The bear appeared suddenly like magic. The ground quaked as he galloped and his paws made thuds as they dug into the gravel road for purchase. I was astonished at his size and shimmering blue-black fur. He left a wake of funky smell, reminiscent of a wet dog with diarrhea. I was too afraid to move; I watched with big eyes as the brush and trees reflected the bear's passage, running down into the valley away from me. I think I asked myself out loud if I was in danger. But the bear was getting farther away each second. After I had collected myself, I rode on down the trail. When I ran into some hikers about a mile later, I was still babbling about seeing a bear.

It took weeks after that first encounter with the black bear to finally get up my courage to go back into the woods alone. In the interim, I started reading about bears and teaching myself to see animal tracks and sign. When I revisited that resting spot, I discovered I had been sitting in the middle of a bear interstate!

On June 12, 1993, I was near Lone Butte Meadows, Washington State, about thirty-five miles from the Columbia River. It was around 8:30 p.m., and I was watching an elk herd. The elk were in the middle of the meadow with new babies. Small elk were butting heads and chasing each other. I watched from a closed road, about fifty feet above the meadow. The herd was relaxed, and I was able to witness this scene because I was alone and quiet. It was a warm, sunny evening with alpenglow tinting Mt. Adams pink in the distance. I inched closer and prepared to sit so I could steady my binoculars. Just then the wind must have changed, or maybe I made a little noise, because a bear mushroomed up like a volcanic cloud from the brush at the edge of the meadow, directly below my position.

I was excited that I was going to get to see a bear running away from me again. I hoped to see it run across the meadow. That's what all the books I had read since my last encounter prepared me to expect. My first impression was the back end of a light-colored bear, about the size of a washing machine. The bear was swallowed up by vegetation as it moved forward, away from me. Using my newly learned skill of scatter vision, I let my eyes bounce easily over the line of brush. No bear appeared. Instead, I heard the sound of cracking sticks. I couldn't tell where it was. Then there was a mysterious stillness that seemed to last for several long minutes as I wondered how something so big could just disappear. Turns out, it had moved stealthily through the brush, doubled back silently, and reappeared about halfway between where I first saw it and where I now stood. It reared up, balancing on hind legs, its nose sniffing audibly. It had a huge head, with very blond ears that impressed me as being small, round, and furry. My subconscious took in the relaxed paws and glittering eyes. I decided this bear had made a simple mistake.

"Hey bear," I yelled toward it with my hand by my mouth, "you're supposed to run away." The bear dropped down to all fours and came ten steps closer, then stood up again. It was then that I decided this light-colored black bear wasn't acting right. I had read that black bears can be any color, so it never occurred to me that I could be interacting with a grizzly in Skamania County, Washington. Plus, everyone knows there are no grizzlies in this area. I looked at the bear and it looked at me. I spoke to it again, "Well, if you're not going to leave, I guess I have to." I turned my head slowly to the side (luckily the right thing to do), and without looking back, moved very cautiously, turning my bike around. I threw a leg over and rode ponderously and nervously away. Expecting to see a furry face in my rearview mirror, I must have left a shaky track.

By the time I got back to my car, I was riding very fast. I shoved my bike in the back, got in, and locked the doors. As I sat there, reviewing the "video clip" of this bear in my memory, it struck me that this light-colored bear had acted very much like the bears I had seen in Alaska.

Three years later, after many calls to various people in the Forest Service, I discovered that a few days before I met with this bear there had been a Class A sighting of a grizzly bear only twelve miles away. "Class A sighting" means it was reported by a reliable Forest Service professional who should know what he saw. The record of my sighting was Class F, I think, if that is what they call the least reliable ones.

When I look back on this experience after spending four summers with brown bears and grizzlies, I realize that this was such a successful encounter because of several things I did by accident. First, I was completely calm. I had taken my eyes off the bear as it was deciding what to do about me, unwittingly giving it the bear body language that I did not want a confrontation. I also moved away with seeming personal power and dignity (definitely by accident). In my favor, too, was the presence of my bike, which was probably something the bear did not feel comfortable about approaching.

Seeing the bear motivated me to study tracking, but this experience launched me into a completely new lifestyle. I began to question everything I thought I knew about the wilderness. I spent as much time as possible out there alone, tracking, watching, and learning.

Chapter Two

Tracking Bears

After reading all the books and literature I could find on bears, I still had one huge question that was not answered satisfactorily. I wanted to know if bears are dangerous to humans. There seemed to be two different sets of books on bears: books in which bears were monsters and books that hinted that bears weren't so bad. My tracking teachers insisted that the truth was spread over the landscape, to be learned through my own observations. Along with reading everything I could find, I went to the woods to study the tracks. For instance, bears can run forty miles per hour, turn over huge boulders, run up almost vertical cliffs, and run down just as fast. They have powerful paws that can dig deep holes and claws that can rip apart trees. Bears can smell things miles away and differentiate between subtle scents to a degree that is hard for us to imagine. In a research paper by Thomas S. Smith, a USGS research wildlife biologist, I read that bears see colors and their hearing is excellent. I tracked a black bear near Sisters,

Oregon, that dug up about twenty acres of terrain, trees, and boulders looking for small mammals. The tracks and dens of the smaller animals were completely obliterated. The strength and physical abilites of the bear were apparent in everything it did. Considering all of this, bears have the potential to be very dangerous indeed.

On the other hand statistically it didn't seem like bears presented much threat to humans. Each year 4.7 million people are bitten by dogs, 6,000 of them need hospitalization, and about 18 of them die. The bear fatality rate, however, is about three people a year in all of North America (including Canada and Alaska). An extensive study was done in the greater Yellowstone area between 1992 and 2000, and it revealed that in thirty-five bear/human encounters thirty-eight people were injured, but no one was killed (approximately three million people visit the park each year). Conversely, seventy-four grizzly bears were killed by human causes during this period. I began to suspect that humans might be the more dangerous animals. The same study also looked at the years from 1975 to 1991: thirty-five injuries and two fatalities, with a rough average of 2 million visitors a year.

The statistics didn't seem to make a difference to writers who were deeply afraid of being mauled by a wild animal, a basic human fear that seems to sell books and movies. When someone does get hurt by a bear, it can be gruesome. The descriptions of mauling injuries and the long, painful recovery time can be heart rending. Early on in my investigations of bear literature I found that the hunting of bears was considered a noble pastime, as it removes threats to the rest of us from the wilderness. This was confusing to me when I read Charlie Russell's first book on bears, *Spirit Bear*. He describes sitting on a log in the Canadian wilderness when a familiar wild grizzly bear sits down with him. They remain quietly side by side, and then she puts her paw on his hand. I had also read Tim Treadwell's book *Living with Grizzlies*, in which he describes camping in grizzly country by himself. Even though I was put off by some of his seemingly childlike ways, I was fascinated by his descriptions of bear behavior.

A research paper by Steven P. French, MD, raised a question that no one seemed to be able to answer: "The point that has puzzled me the most is not that grizzlies occasionally prey on humans, but why they don't do it more often. As a potential prey species, humans are predictable and abundant, are easy to catch and easy to kill, and are very easy to consume for a grizzly. So why don't they prey on us as part of their routine feeding behavior?"

I finally decided I would have to answer the question for myself. By tracking bears, I could learn more about their behavior. In the past, whenever I had been afraid of something, it was a sign that I needed to know more about it.

Learning to track bears is easier said than done. Bears have wide, soft paws that leave indistinct impressions. In our environment here in the Pacific Northwest there are lots of tracks of deer and elk, which leave deep, sharp impressions in the forest duff. Almost anyone can track them because they are like following a lady in high heels. Bears are not as numerous and are often shy.

I was lucky to have two encounters with bears when I wasn't expecting them. Shortly after, when I was looking everywhere for bear tracks, it seemed they had all disappeared. By fall I had a new strategy. Bears leave striking berry scats in the fall, easily detected by riding a mountain bike down closed roads. I would ride until I found a fresh pile that looked like someone had dropped a huckleberry pie in the road and then get off my bike and look for tracks.

Sometimes it took many minutes for me to discern the subtle marks of the track. Then I would mark it with a colored popsicle stick and try to find the next one. When I had a few marked, I would stand back and see if I could discern the pattern. Bears usually make a wide path, and when you know what to look for, they make quite a bit of disturbance in the vegetation. However, they can also walk in a stealthy manner, putting one paw in the same spot another just vacated, making a straight, soft trail. I discovered that bears don't walk down the road, but meander alongside it, casually leaving a scat and then wandering indirectly back into cover. Months of discovery uncovered lots of different behaviors without the sighting of an actual bear. I found bear hair on trees, scratch marks, digging spots, and the remnants of different types of meals.

Following bear trails gave me a different opinion of the animal. I started to appreciate how it must feel not to be able to go to Safeway and stock up. I was in awe of the way a bear could disappear from sight in vegetation and how close they could come to humans without being detected. I found their day beds and lay down in them, trying to find out what it would feel like to be a bear. I would sit in a bear resting spot for long periods of time and listen to what they hear and look at the good view they would almost always pick out for their spots. A couple of times someone did walk by when I was in a bear daybed. Just like a bear, I felt the need to stay hidden and stayed low and motionless until the people were safely past.

During the time I was learning to see animal tracks, I was invited to join search and rescue in our area. As soon as I learned that searchers could go to tracking classes I was all for it. My first human tracking class, with Universal Tracking Service in Oregon, was astounding. I met Joel Hardin, a former border patrol tracker, and his team, and they opened my eyes to new tracking possibilities. I also got a hint of tracking politics when I mentioned my first tracking teacher, the books of Tom Brown. Apparently, I made a faux pas. Back in the early nineties, the tracking world was strictly split between animal trackers and human trackers. Animal trackers were interested in seeing gaits and clear tracks in what we call "track traps," spots of mud or sand where tracks register well. Human trackers were interested in following the tracks and being able to see tracks in any substrate. I decided that both skills were mandatory for me and applied myself to learning to follow tracks as well as gaining as much knowledge as I could from animal trackers.

After a few enlightening human tracking classes in which I learned to see subtle color changes, small broken sticks, misplaced pebbles, dirt transfer, and many other details, I had a bear tracking revelation. I was in the Gifford Pinchot National Forest in Washington when I found a fresh pile of bear scat. I found the first two bear paw prints by using my handheld mirror to manipulate the light and create shadows in the toe impressions of the track. Soon the bear tracks wandered off the road and I used a Joel Hardin trick to see where it entered the thick vegetation. There was a heavy dew on most of the leaves, but one section was dry. Parting the weeds gently with my tracking stick I found a relatively clear trail to follow. I stepped down into the deep cover and tracked the bear about a hundred yards until I was unsure of just where he had stepped next. I looked around, suspecting that the bear was still in the area. I also realized that I had been so focused on the tracks that I had been pretty quiet. For some reason, I picked up a stick and cracked it in half. I stood still and listened. A stick cracking just down the slope from me let me know where the bear was. I looked in that direction and noticed a large fungus on a log, which had a clear bear track in the middle of it. The fungus was visibly returning to its original shape. I decided to leave.

About a month later, a bear crossed in front of me when I was driving a back road. I parked the car and got out to look at his tracks. After I found his trail I advanced one track at a time, trying to learn as much as I could from each track. I forgot about the bear. When I heard a stick crack, it got my attention. The noise wasn't close, so I cracked a stick, too, and kept tracking. Soon another stick cracked a little further away. I answered in kind. Within a minute I heard him answer. I was comfortable with this "stick game" and assumed the bear was too, until he pushed down a dead tree. His point of superior strength had been made and I backed off.

I was getting better at spotting bear tracks by the time I went to Yellowstone National Park to take a class on animal tracking with Dr. James Halfpenny. The class revealed more bear behavior to me in a different habitat. One of the keys to animal track identification is to study the gait. This class gave a great foundation in putting the tracking story together using gait and track placement. Dr. Halfpenny had a wealth of naturalist knowledge based on his own scientific studies, and seeing bear tracks in Yellowstone showed me that bear behavior is closely related to what bears have to eat. There is a vast difference in the mood of a hungry bear and one who is full with plenty of food around for later snacks.

On a summer evening near my home, I passed what I considered to be the bear tracking test. I was early to a search and rescue training campout and decided to look around before the others got there. I found a dead tree that had clear bear claw marks where a black bear had been pulling off the rotten wood to get to the bug feast inside. At the base of the tree were the wide, soft signature impressions of a bear's front paws. When the others arrived and we set up camp, I asked two of our members, who were also avid hunters, if they wanted to see some bear tracks. These two guys, Keith and Kent Lay, were twins and the epitome of outdoor "mountain men." They could start a fire in wet snow in minutes and knew more about the woods than anyone I had met. At first they couldn't see the tracks, and for a second I wondered if I was wrong. I used a stick and slowly showed them the outlines until the tracks jumped out at them. I think I earned their respect just then and had passed my test.

I was starting to feel comfortable with the idea of sharing the woods peacefully with the black bears in the area. I had decided that being calm in the presence of bears was key. I was able to put that theory to the test the next summer. My friend Ellen and I were partially concealed in the long grass of a remote meadow watching a herd of elk graze. When it was time to leave, we stood up and moved a little way back up the slope. We were admiring the mountain view when Ellen said urgently in my ear, "There is a bear." I asked her where and leaned closer to her so I could share her view. About fifty yards from us was a gorgeous black bear standing sideways to show us his size. I said, "Cool," and Ellen said, "I guess so."

This was before I had spent time in Alaska with bears, so I didn't consider his big yawn as a passive-aggressive sign. Then he started moving in our direction at a somewhat leisurely pace. Ellen said "He's coming right toward us." I responded, "Yeah, isn't that cool?" She moved so she was just a little behind my left shoulder and murmured, "I guess so." I watched calmly as the bear approached to about ten steps from us and then wrinkled up his long snout and took a big sniff. "Yuk," he seemed to say. He swung his head sideways and moved away from us with a definite attitude. He did a cool-dude slouch, a walk with a little back swing in it.

Ellen asked "What should we do now?" I said we should give him a little time and let him go where he wants. After about ten minutes we moved back up the slope to our mountain bikes and walked them out toward the main road. Halfway there, I asked Ellen if she wanted to see him again. I pointed out the bear standing on his hind legs inside the branches of a fir tree with his arms wrapped around the trunk. He was watching us and thought he was invisible, but he was so big his back end was sticking out. I told Ellen it was our turn to give him the same cool exit walk he had given us to watch. We pushed our bikes with a swagger, tossing our hair.

That encounter made me think that being in direct sight of a bear might be an important factor. In other words, a bear can know you are there by your smell, your sound, and your tracks, but if you keep out of sight, it may not be forced to deal with you in a defensive manner. I think this incident was the first one that led me to believe that bears communicate with body language as well as smell.

A month later I saw the same bear again, feeding in a field of clover. I was across the meadow from him on a hillside, at what I thought was a safe distance. After almost two hours of watching him graze in a big circle and look everywhere else, I deduced that he must have known I was there. I was interested in his response, but didn't know how common it was until I had more experience. Much later, in Alaska, I realized that bears who pretend they don't see you are sending a message.

By about 1999 I had gained a reputation as a tracker who could answer questions about animals. One of my first animal tracking calls came from Keith Lay. He was acting as the caretaker of the Girl Scout camp near my home in Washington State in a remote little valley by the Columbia River. The camp is in a horizontal slide, an unusual geological area that has earth movement sideways instead of down. Located between Wind Mountain and Dog Mountain, it also has dozens of little lakes. It's covered with thick vegetation and some parts are hard to get to because the trails and roads aren't always in the same place year after year. Consequently, it is a haven for wildlife as well as an ideal spot for Girl Scouts to have an outdoor adventure. Northeast of the camp is a range of foothills to the Cascade Mountains, which stretch from Canada south into Oregon. These mountains make a good wildlife corridor, sometimes allowing animals to travel south from as far away as the Canadian border.

Although I wasn't surprised to get the call from Keith, I was concerned about his description of the bear's behavior. Campers had encountered the bear in broad daylight and had banged pans and thrown objects at it, but it didn't run away. This worried everyone. It concerned me because the black bears in the area are known to be very elusive and usually run at the first signs of humans. From the descriptions of the bear, including its color and behavior, I thought there might be a slight chance that a traveling teenage grizzly bear was in the area. After I had seen a grizzly in the state, I found references to other bears who had wandered that far.

I agreed to track the bear and try to figure out what was going on. It didn't take me long to pick up the bear's tracks just outside the dining hall. I followed them along the ridges and into thick brush. Keith joined me, and between us, we were able to get pretty close to the animal. At one juncture, we came upon a rotted stump full of frenzied ants that had just been raked by the claws of the bear. We found spots where the bear had rested, and uncovered left-over wrappers from sandwiches that Girl Scouts had left lying around. After a while Keith needed to get back to his chores so I carried on alone. I found that the bear had many secluded resting spots that were just out of sight. I followed the pushed-down vegetation to a narrow ridge where the bear had a little nest behind a downed tree. When I stooped to check out what the bear could see from there, I saw a clearing just below the ridge with a campfire ring and rustic log seats. It was probably a place where nighttime singing and camp activities took place. The bear had a great view of the whole thing. The little nest with a view also had residue from human snack food. There was even marshmallow on the vegetation.

When I had tracked the bear's activity in a circle around every camp space, I found myself close to the staff office. There, just across the creek, was the bear's main hideout. The remnants of every kind of Girl Scout treat were mashed into the flattened long grass, and tufts of bear fur were dangling from the brush.

After a thorough examination of the bear's "living room," I headed to a meeting with the staff. I explained what I had learned about the bear and then recommended that they call in the Fish and Wildlife officers to trap and relocate the bear. Everyone agreed that the bear was being too bold. Based on its patterns of movement, I thought that it was probably a young bear recently separated from its mother. The bear probably found the Girl Scout camp and figured he was in heaven. Songs, games, and lots of snacks were perfect for a lonely cub that needed a new home.

I forgot about the bear for a few days, but about four days later, I got another phone call. Keith said that the Fish and Wildlife officer had tried everything, but they couldn't get the bear into the trap. I asked what they were using for bait and was informed it was the usual stuff: stinky chicken, hamburger, and fish. I thought a minute and realized what the problem was. "Put in Little Debbies," I advised. Every bear bed I had found had Little Debbie wrappers. A couple of hours later, I was in a class when my cell phone rang. Keith said they had the bear and were going to relocate him in the morning.

After tracking the bear for a day, I really wanted to see what it looked like, so after class my friend Ellen and I stopped by the Girl Scout camp. As we approached the wagon with the trap on it, I suddenly wished I wasn't a tracker. I could see lug boot prints and sharpened sticks lying in a circle around the cage. It was obvious that someone had been prodding and teasing the bear. The trap was located just outside the camp gates, so it was accessible to anyone. The bear was huddled and shaking in the darkest back corner of the trap. It was a warm summer evening, about eleven at night. I wanted to get a look at the bear, so Ellen and I sat down on the on the trap's wagon hitch, right by the front of the cage. We started talking softly between ourselves. We talked about the last bear we had seen together and how we would feel being in the cage. We were ready to give the bear some time to get used to our presence. We purposely didn't peer into the cage but just acted as if we were sitting on a country fence, waiting for the moon to come up.

Finally, we could sense the bear calming down and sliding forward little by little. In about forty minutes, he was closer to us and was making a humming noise, like little cubs do when they're nursing. We tried humming songs, too. Soon the bear was licking his paws and acting relaxed. I was able to get a close look at the face and paws and determined that it was a black bear. Ellen and I hated to leave but it was getting very late, and the sleepy attitude of the bear was making us wish for our own beds.

I woke up very early the next morning and hoped to see the bear again before it was relocated. I threw on my clothes, shook my husband Mike from a deep sleep, and convinced him to go with me. We drove straight to the spot where the trap had been the night before, but the Fish and Wildlife officer had been up even earlier. The bear and trap were gone.

When I caught up with the officer later, I asked him how the release went. He said he took the bear up near Mt. Adams and the Yakima Indian Reservation, and that the transfer went smoothly, although the bear hesitated just a little leaving the trap. After the officer chased it out, the bear walked about ten feet and sat down, turning around to look at the officer over its shoulder. I always wondered if the bear, which just wanted to be a Girl Scout, was as mystified about people as they were about him. This bear never returned to the camp, maybe because it had been transported back to near where it was raised. Bears, just like people, have regional differences. For example, the black bears from the the Yakima area have a propensity to be a particular color that I would call burnt sienna. Some of them look like dark-haired people who have tried to dye their hair blond, resulting in a dull reddish color. The Girl Scout camp bear had that color.

The next call I got was from a farm manager who called me to track a bear that had killed some goats. I couldn't get there for a few days; and by the time I had arrived, a neighbor had shot the bear. I went out to look for the tracks anyway. I was directed to the spot where the bear had been shot, which was in a clearing where they kept the beehives. Bees were plentiful that day, and I got to practice my theory of quiet, slow movements around animals in order not to get hurt. As I found the kill site, the bees were all over me happily checking me out. The Fish and Wildlife Department had removed the bear carcass.

On first my first examination of the site, I found that the bear was indeed guilty of tearing up a beehive and carrying it off into the nearby woods to consume. He had come back for a second portion when he was killed. I picked up his trail from his resting spot near the hives and followed it backward into the woods between the farms. I spent a couple of hours following his meandering, casual trail until he crossed the road into some really thick growth. There I stooped and crawled through a tunnel bear trail until I came to a tree den where this animal had obviously been spending quite a bit of time. I was expecting to find the remains of the missing goats in the bear's scat. I dissected the most recent sample and found only berries and grasses. I spent another two hours following the animal's trails but none of them came near the farm where the goats were missing.

Thinking I might have missed something, I returned to the farm and started from the goat pen. The only tracks I found were those of a big dog. I backtracked them toward the house of the neighbor who had shot the bear. His dogs were penned up when I went by. It was time to quit for the day, and I went home wondering what had really happened to the goats. Since the bear was already dead, I thought that looking into it further wouldn't be necessary. If the bear was the culprit, the rest of the goats were safe. If not, time would tell. The relations between neighbors were already delicate, so I left the whole thing alone.

By 2000 I felt I knew a little bit about black bears. I had tracked them, seen them, and read everything I could find about them. Of course, when you think you know something, that is the time you should really pay attention. It was a Saturday morning when I got a callout for a bear mauling. The Skamania County sheriff's office had requested the assistance of Wind River Search and Rescue, of which I am a member. When Wind River receives a call, one member does a "callout," dialing about sixty phone numbers and explaining the situation to each person, just giving you the briefest facts. You have a minute or so to decide whether you will respond. The deputy in charge of the mission needs to know how many volunteers he can count on for planning purposes. I said I would be there and started to get ready.

As I grabbed fresh water and snacks to add to the loaded pack in my Subaru, I couldn't help thinking about those two words: "bear mauling." The scene of the attack was close to where I live, only about ten miles as the crow flies, but on the winding, twisting dirt tracks it took forty minutes to get there. As I drove the familiar roads, I had a sense of dread. I was very curious as to how someone managed to get mauled by one of the shy, reclusive black bears of Washington State, but I was also steeling myself for the sight of some horrible injuries.

When I arrived at the scene there were rescue vehicles, ambulances, police cars, and Department of Fish and Wildlife trucks parked alongside my teammates' cars on a narrow dirt road on the side of a steep slope. I had to park down the road a bit.

As I signed in, the deputy in charge told me that my team had already set up a rope system to haul the subject up. The system was anchored to one of the trucks on the road with a main rope and belay. The team at the bottom would be packaging the subject in a stokes, a stretcher basket that is attached to the ropes and guided up by climbers. The team at the top hauls the whole group up with a pulley system. In this case, even though it was steep, they were set up for a low-angle rescue. Even though search and rescue is a volunteer activity, most of our members are highly trained specialists, purchasing their own gear and taking time out of their lives to become competent to help others.

Everyone seemed a little subdued at the rescue base so I waited for an assignment quietly. The Fish and Wildlife officer approached me and asked if I would look for any tracks or sign that might support the subject's story. When I track a lost person, I always want to know as much as I can find out about the person before I start, and asking questions in base camp is part of the tracker's job; but since this was a different kind of tracking I thought it would be best not to know exactly what I was looking for so that I would have no expectations. When you look for a story on the ground, it often reveals itself to you more clearly if you are not expecting to see certain things. I didn't realize that my overactive imagination had already created some expectations.

I strapped on my pack and headed to the area the officer indicated might yield some tracks. As I worked, I listened my rescue radio. The team was being very quiet and the only thing I heard from them was the "reset" and "set" commands as they hauled the subject up the slope. The eerie silence of the crew made me glad I wasn't on the ropes system, as I figured it meant they were dealing with some very serious injuries.

Soon my attention was totally engaged by the "story on the road." What I saw made no sense. There were clear tracks from a black bear cub in a sandy culvert on the uphill side of the road right next to some obvious canine tracks. The dog had thrown some sand out of its track depressions, which had landed in the interdigital pads of the bear's front paw prints. That meant that this little bear was probably being chased by the dog. One of the harder distinctions in tracking is between domestic dogs and wild canines. Well-fed dogs have splayed-out toes indicating a soft lifestyle, while wild dogs have well-exercised feet that show the front toes pulled in. In this case it was a toss up, as the animal was running on a soft substrate that might spread out the toes of a wild canine.

I took some digital pictures, and then went back to the road to look for the mother bear tracks and the tracks of the injured man. I scanned the road dust, the shoulder dust, and the vegetation on the sides of the road and looked for plant disturbance, blood spots, and flies. I saw a very obvious area of pushed down-brush headed straight down the steep slope almost across from the cub tracks I had found. I carefully stepped down and saw some indistinct boot tracks indicated by a mashed and torn thistle plant. This sign appeared to continue down the slope, but it looked like the person wasn't standing for the rest of it, but possibly sliding on his back end. This slide mark would have obscured any bear tracks that were under it, and I could tell it would be a one-way trip if I went down further. It was too slippery to climb back up. The roadside was full of tire marks of various vehicles and a few boot tracks but only in the immediate area. The dusty road was an easy tracking surface, but I still couldn't find the tracks I expected to see: those of a bigger bear.

Finally, I returned to the clear tracks in the culvert and back-tracked them up a little canyon to a very dense wooded area above the road. Interestingly, there was only the one set of bear tracks along with canine tracks.

By the time I made my way back to the base, the team was almost to the road with the subject and everyone was still quiet. They transferred the subject quickly to the waiting ambulance, which took off immediately. The team rested and drank water while I reported to the Fish and Wildlife officer. I assumed that the cub I had tracked was with a mother bear and that if the mother was involved in a mauling, the poor cub was now separated and running around lost.

That's when I got the story. The officer asked me to look in the back of his truck. There was the cub. It was dead; its little paws were a perfect match for the tracks I had seen. The cub was about the size of a German shepherd. I asked the officer, "Is *this* the bear?" He nodded. "How could this little bear maul somebody badly enough to be taken to the hospital?" I asked. Some of my dusty, tired team members ducked their heads quickly and looked away.

Apparently, the injured man was hunting for bears and shot this bear as it crossed the road. No dogs were involved, because hunting with dogs is illegal. The man wounded the bear on the road, then followed it down the canyon walls, tramped all around, and finally stepped on the bush the bear was in, where-upon the bear bit his ankle and held on like a puppy dog. The man pulled out his extra gun, a Colt .45, and shot at the bear and missed, hitting his own foot. He then fell on the bear and the bear died.

The man's hunting buddies were listening to this as it was quietly related to me. I tried to remain passive as I asked the officer if he thought this was a first-year cub. I expressed that I thought it might be. The officer said they would pull a tooth and find out, but when I walked away, the guys yelled at me that I couldn't know anything about bears if I thought that was a cub of the year. They maintained that it was a two-year-old separated from its mother and therefore was legal to shoot. When I disagreed (when will I ever learn!) they became much more animated about it. So, I thought it best to beat a hasty retreat. I got into my car and drove back to town. In retrospect, they could have been right, but it was a close call. It was late August, and a single cub of the year could have gotten that big if he had a good mother and a plentiful berry crop.

When I got to town, I stopped in the bakery where my team had gathered to debrief. They had had a very hard morning. The man was no lightweight, and even though his injuries weren't what we expected, they were serious. Interestingly, the injured hunter was on the eleven o'clock news from his hospital bed, heroically promising that as soon as he was better he would be back out hunting those fierce bears so the rest of us could be safe. This incident went on the record as a "bear mauling," as the bear did leave a couple of teeth marks. The true nature of the injury to the man's foot was never made public.

I was beginning to wonder about bear mauling. Kent Lay had quietly investigated another incident in Klickitat County where a hunter was allegedly attacked by a black bear. The victim was scratched and bruised and had a wild tale to tell. Kent said that the tracks indicated the hunter had run after seeing a bear, and fell down into a nasty barbed-wire-laden ditch trying to get away. Whether the bear was running after him or away from him was still a question.

It was around this time that I heard another "bear attack" story from a fish biologist. I don't know if it's true, partly true, or just a good story, but it is illustrative of the bears' side of things. Two fish biologists were working a remote stream in bear country. They were walking the stream bed in chest waders and taking temperatures and samples of the water, one behind the other. The young man in front was an apprentice (we'll call him Joe) and the biologist bringing up the rear (we'll call him Bob) was an experienced woods person. Because they were in the water, their smell was obscured, and the stream was covering the sounds they made. Inevitably, the came by a spot on the bank where a black bear was sleeping. Joe turned and yelled a question to Bob, and his voice woke up the bear. When Joe turned back around, he saw the bear, about fifteen feet from him. He started yelling "Bear!" and backing up, splashing the water with his hands. Bob was watching the bear, who rubbed his sleepy head with a paw in an effort to wake up and understand what was happening. Joe must have missed this clue; he continued to get agitated.

As Bob watched, the bear widened his eyes and looked into the woods behind himself, turning both ways. Then he looked back at Joe for a moment before he sprang up and took off at full speed in Joe's direction. Of course, all Joe saw at this point was a bear coming straight toward him. Joe slipped on the slimy stream bottom and fell into the water, going completely under as the bear sped past him and raced into the woods on the opposite side of the stream. The bear had probably figured Joe was no threat to him, while whatever it was that had scared Joe in the woods behind the bear must be really dangerous. When Joe came up sputtering, he fully believed he had been knocked down by the bear and didn't understand why Bob just couldn't stop laughing. It is too bad for Joe that there was a witness, as his version sure would have made a good story back at the bar.

The bears I have tracked and studied over the years don't think of themselves as scary. Bears don't watch the movies of themselves as monsters growling, drooling, and swiping things with massive paws. Instead, they grow up being submissive to older bears and take great care not to put themselves in danger. They move through the landscape quietly, cautiously, and with attention to the details. On top of that, bears have no reason to believe that we are weaklings. After all, we smell strongly of rich foods like great hunters, and we are tall and imposing in our insolent way of making lots of noise and walking a direct path. I have watched bears become incredibly frightened when a person near them panics. Years after I heard the fish biologist's story, after guiding lots of people in bear country, I have found that it takes practice on the part of a human to even notice the body language of a bear. When I have asked people to reconstruct their own body language during an encounter, that too was elusive for them.

Although biologists think bears have a chase impulse similar to dogs, it's possible that running from a bear encounter in a frenzy of fear instigates contact between humans and bears just because of infectious pandemonium. I suspected that there are innocent bears who have been convicted of heinous crimes due to misunderstanding.

As I tracked and learned about animals, I also learned that there are politics attached to bears, wolves, lynx, and cougars. In 1993 the official word from government agencies was that we didn't have grizzly bears in Washington State. When I saw one and reported it, I was made to understand that I was probably a little irrational at the time of the bear sighting and couldn't have known what I was seeing. Unfortunately, I learned the hard way not to tell people about wildlife I encountered. So now, when I see a wolf, lynx, grizzly bear, or cougar, or unmistakable tracks where they shouldn't be, I keep quiet. Either they don't believe me (like my Class F sighting), or worse, they go out and do the old "shoot, shovel, and shut up," and then the animal is gone.

Over time tracking became a way of life for me, and there wasn't anywhere I walked that I wasn't aware of the movement of living things on the land. With all my observations I discovered that biologists, naturalists, and casual observers think things about animals that have been passed around as common knowledge but aren't always true. In the summer of 2000 I took part in a predator survey in the Gifford Pinchot National Forest. We set up remote motion-sensing cameras, scent lures, and tracking traps to capture paw prints. Everything we expected to find was elusive, but some of the things we did find were almost unbelievable. At one tracking station, miles from any civilization, we found a thriving black rooster. Lynx are not expected to be found below four thousand feet in elevation, but I found one happily eating the snowshoe hares, which weren't supposed to be there either, at twenty-eight hundred feet. I had learned that being a tracker was a true way to understand the ever-changing wild world, and I fully expected to be able to answer my questions about bears. I just needed to get some time in grizzly bear country.

In 2001 my husband and I decided to change our lifestyles. The idea of working in Alaska seemed logical. Mike had worked in the resort business for years and was also a fine finish carpenter with many talents. I still had my 100-Ton Coast Guard captain's license, plus a new awareness of the natural world. I found Within the Wild Alaskan Adventure Lodges, a company that owned three Alaskan lodges, on the Internet and talked to the owners by phone. Our combination of experience was perfect. We were an ideal match. Mike and I would become the managing couple of Redoubt Bay Lodge, a remote, fly-in only, bear-viewing lodge. And just like that we packed up our stuff and headed north for the adventure of a lifetime.

Chapter Three

Summer 2002

We arrived in Anchorage in the middle of the night, as do many people who fly there. It wasn't completely dark out but merely dim. Our new company had booked us into a hotel, and it was about 2:00 A.M. when we finally checked in. In the morning I opened the curtain to get my first-ever view of Anchorage. I saw a chain-link fence and a junkyard dog. Mike and I found this so humorous we took a picture. Two hours later, we met with our new bosses, and any doubts about working for people we had only met on the phone disappeared. Carl and Kirsten Dixon ran a professional organization that far exceeded our expectations.

Right away, we were eager to board a floatplane and get to the lodge. However, there was one small problem: The lodge was still snowed in and the lake was frozen. But Riversong Lodge, another lodge owned by the company, was accessible and needed lots of work before opening. So we left Anchorage on a partly cloudy, windy day and headed for Riversong with a planeload of supplies.

The floatplane struggled against the wind as it traveled up Yentna River valley. My nose made prints on the window as I watched the sandbars scroll by, searching for tracks from five hundred feet up. I was looking for bears everywhere.

During our stay at Riversong I went for hikes on the trails behind the lodge. There were recent bear tracks there, so I figured a bear might be watching me. Since I was by myself, I tried the stick-cracking trick that had worked for me in Washington State. Every few minutes I would pick up a small branch and break it. My theory, from watching bears react to that sound, is that in bear language this means something like "I am a big bad bear and I don't care if you know where I am." Although I didn't spot a bear, I heard one step on a stick and crack it. In this way I knew its location and could avoid passing too close for its comfort.

Soon we heard that the ice had cleared from Big River Lake and we could fly to Redoubt Bay Lodge. The winter caretaker was ready to leave after being there eight months by himself, and we were anxious to get settled in our summer home. We couldn't wait to see brown bears in their natural, wild habitat.*

By 2002 some great work had been done in the field with bears. Several naturalists and biologists had taken the study of bears to an up-close-and-personal level. Charlie Russell and Maureen

---

* While both "grizzly" and "brown" are accurate common names for the species *Ursus arctos horribilis*, the difference is that coastal bears in Alaska are called brown bears, and interior bears are grizzly bears. Browns are bigger, eat more salmon, and have a nicer disposition as a result of being full most of the time. Grizzlies who don't have access to as much protein are smaller and have a reputation for being less tolerant. The bears near Redoubt Bay Lodge have salmon and tolerate humans, but they are smaller than brown bears. They also spend time twenty to thirty miles from the coast, and brown bears are usually within twenty miles of the coast. Although either name could suit the Redoubt Bay bears, I chose to call them brown bears in this book since their behavior more closely resembles that of brown bears.

Enns were raising grizzly cubs in the wilds of Kamchatka Peninsula in Russia. Dr. Steve Stringham had raised some black bear
cubs, which he wrote about in *Beauty Within the Beast.* Benjamin
Kilham's new book about raising wild cubs had just come out, and
I had taken a copy to Alaska with me. My own observations of
black bears had made me intensely curious about the brown bear
population in Alaska. I hoped for an open "tracker's mind" that
would allow me to make fresh observations.

The flight to Big River Lakes from Riversong Lodge is spectac-
ular, although it was too cloudy for us to take the scenic mountain
route. As soon as we were airborne, I started looking for animals.
I pointed out a black bear on a hillside to the pilot, and he circled
around to give us a good view (and queasy stomachs). As we neared
the lodge, we flew over some perfect bear habitat: rivers and
mountains with secluded, inaccessible valleys and different elevations full of diverse plants. The lodge is located on Big River Lake
on a hill that has a great view. Planes fly in from the east, following Big River to the lake over tidal flats and floating bogs. As you
approach the lodge from the air, it looks like it is nestled in the
outstretched arms of rugged, snowy mountains and glaciers. Five
other lakes in the area are connected to the main lake by creeks.
The central bear-viewing spot, Wolverine Cove, is about a mile
from the lodge, across the lake.

The dock was still iced in, so we had to park the plane at the
bank in front of the main lodge building. Amidst the unloading
of the plane and the bustle to get the winter caretaker aboard, I
stumbled across the clearest, deepest bear tracks I had seen since
the Lamar River in Yellowstone. I bent down and put my hand in
one of the tracks. It was deep, wide, and had the signature toe
alignment that meant it was a brown bear. I thought of the animal

that had stepped right there, just outside the cabin in which Mike and I would sleep all summer. I realized how lucky I was to have the opportunity to be closer to understanding the mystery and connection I had felt with the Lone Butte bear.

Over the next week we worked hard to get the lodge into shape for summer guests. I couldn't help but look up every few minutes to scan the lake shore. I investigated every pushed-down plant and turned leaf. I saw signs of bears but couldn't catch a glimpse of one.

Finally, with binoculars trained on the far shore of the lake, I spied a brown bear moving along the bear trail. That first bear I spotted that day became a regular sighting. She was a young bear that seemed to be wandering aimlessly around the lake. We would glimpse her jumping over a log on the bear trail, then later watch her swim from bog to bog. In the morning we would see her tracks through the lodge campus, evidence of her quiet passage while we were sleeping. This little blond bear was to play an important role in my first three years as a bear viewing guide. The Washington State University researchers who were there that year named her Emma.

Soon salmon were swimming in the main lake and the glaciers around the area had started to melt, making the lake turn a beautiful, soft, slate green. Mike and I were focused on learning how to run a wilderness lodge; and before we knew it, the plants were shoulder high and the lodge was full of visitors coming and going. After all that searching for bears, they came to us, both at the lodge and doing their annual fishing at Wolverine Cove. By the middle of June, I had spent several long days watching bears and felt my learning curve had taken a dramatic upswing.

Overall, 2002 was an outstanding bear viewing year, thanks to a young mother bear and her three tiny cubs. One of the researchers named her Baylee after one of his daughters. Baylee was a sterling example of bear motherhood. Her three cubs were seldom more than five feet from her. When she started fishing in Wolverine Cove, she would place them on the rocks with a motherly "huff huff." After every dive she would look up to make sure they were all right. Watching Baylee, and her three cubs of the year ("coys" in bearspeak), was a daily treat.

I discovered that the Wolverine Cove bears make several distinct noises. What I call the "huffing" noise seems to be only between cubs and mothers. Another sound, a blowing or woofing that is sometimes accompanied by a popping noise, indicates a very nervous bear, or one who feels he is being threatened. Guests often ask why the bears are generally so quiet. They expected roaring and growling, I think, and the huffing a mother bear makes is subtle and can be easily missed if you aren't listening for it. But little bears pay strict attention to that noise. Sometimes they will run after the mother when she does it, and other times they will stay put like puppies who have been disciplined. There are nuances to the sound, but I was never able to detect them. After a few years, I surmised that "huffing" is coupled with other body language that provides the little ones further instructions.

The research group from Washington State University had set up a safe viewing tower in Wolverine Cove in order to make observations twenty-four hours a day. They chose to name the bears in the area as well as give them identification numbers. This proved to be a bonus for us, because using bear names between guides was a quick way to transfer information. For instance, if a guide called and said Mona was fishing, we all knew how slow she was and we could judge whether we could get to the location in time to see her. As the summer wore on, the names took on more meaning as we became familiar with the habits and personalities of each bear.

Sometime during the summer, Baylee started to look me directly in the eyes. I had read that making eye contact with a bear was at least impolite, if not downright aggressive. My relationship with Baylee took a dramatic shift soon after that. One day she was resting on the rocks near the head of the stream, a place bears would sprawl between periods of fishing in the cove. I had anchored one of the pontoon boats with some guests nearby. She kept gazing at me intently. I returned her gaze calmly, as if mother bears stared at me every day. Finally, she huffed at the cubs and they sat down on the spot, shooting me nervous glances. They stretched their little bodies toward Baylee as she took off, slipping into the thick vegetation where we couldn't see her anymore. She had left the cubs!

In about twenty minutes (which seemed like hours), Baylee appeared at the edge of the brush. She huffed at the cubs. They jumped up, tumbling and scrambling over the rocks to meet her. They all rubbed noses and then went about their bear business, eventually moving off up the trail.

Baylee left her cubs with me five times before I realized it was intentional (and before I wondered how much she was willing to pay me for these services). Once, I had to call the lodge and ask a pilot to wait for the guests. When I said we were babysitting cubs, I got a gruff answer. The pilots were definitely starting to wonder about me. Luckily, slightly "off" people are pretty well accepted in Alaska.

Baylee taught me something different from what I had learned in the books. When she looked me in the eyes it didn't necessarily mean that she was ready to charge me. That first summer only Baylee gazed at me directly. As I became more familiar with other bears, some of them would make eye contact as well. They may have assumed I understood their nuances, and sometimes I *could* actually get a sense of what they wanted, especially if they used other overt behaviors anyone could figure out (for example, slapping a paw down to underline an aggressive look).

Baylee developed intense relationships with several people, and one of them was photographer Amy Shapira. Even when I had other guests on my boat, Baylee was particularly aware of Amy. In many of Amy's photographs of Baylee there is a sense of this alert interaction. I will never forget Baylee standing on the rocks gazing directly at Amy while we motored out of the cove to meet Amy's floatplane that would take her home. Amy was in tears, and Baylee, however unprofessional it may seem to say so, appeared to share her sadness and understand her reluctance to leave.

Mona, another mature female bear, also taught me something important that first year. One guest asked me if it was true that brown bears didn't climb trees. Since that is what I had read in numerous books, I told the guest it was true, adding some logical reasons. For example, browns are heavier and their claws are not curved like black bear claws; therefore, they don't climb trees. But within forty minutes of my explanation, Mona appeared near the cove and climbed up a spruce tree. She stayed there, swaying in the breeze, until we all noticed her. I couldn't help but think she was mocking me. The tree climbing behavior was further confirmed when I observed Emma in trees several times. Some of my guests were surprised one day as we watched a bald eagle at the top of the ridge perched in a spruce tree. A guest scanned the rest of the tree with binoculars and discovered three brown bears perched at different levels. The bears seemed to be checking out whatever had drawn the eagle there. So next time someone asked me a question about bears, I wasn't so quick to regurgitate unverified "facts."

Emma, who was probably three years old in 2002, was a favorite sighting. Bears are chased away from their mothers at the beginning of their third summer. They reach sexual maturity about their fifth summer. Three-year-old bears are the equivalent of teenagers, and Emma was very entertaining with her antics. On a sunny, cool July afternoon, Emma was trying to catch a salmon in Wolverine Cove. There were lots of boats full of human fishermen trying to work the same spot. Most of the time fishermen stop fishing if one of the larger mother bears wades into the pool. This smaller three-year-old walked into the water among the boats, just as she had seen the big bears do, but the humans didn't give her the same respect. The guides picked up their paddles and moved toward her with a threatening attitude to scoot her away from the concentration of salmon.

There is a spot in the cove that fisherman call the "honey hole," where anyone can catch a salmon. It's a deeper hole where the salmon gather before they make the final run up Wolverine Creek to the lake where they will spawn. It is also where a bear can trap a salmon in its paws because the salmon are packed tightly together. As a group of guests and I watched the fishermen prepare to shoo Emma away, we noticed a sudden attitude shift in her. She bounced out of the water and shook herself dry. Over her shoulder she assessed the situation with a look I can only describe as hostile. Then, tossing her head, Emma exited the cove area to the left. She started moving east on the bear trail at a pretty good pace. We picked up anchor and followed at a distance, just to see what she would do. She ran past what we call the eagle tree, a place that marks the end of the cove area. Emma pushed through brush, jumped over logs, and splashed through the water sections, making good time. I had to speed up to keep her in sight. We could hear branches cracking under her weight and see the steam from her breath. At the end of the lakeside section of the trail, Emma came upon an empty fishing boat pulled up on shore. We arrived just in time to see her use a forepaw to give the boat a mighty whack that echoed across the lake. Next, she pushed the boat up so it was resting on its side, as if she was going to turn it over. Then she let it drop. After doing that a couple of times, she jumped into the boat and threw out the gas can and some cushions. When she attacked the oars they made a cracking sound as they splintered into pieces.

At this point she looked up and saw that she had an audience. My boat had been joined by one of the other guide boats. The other guide and I wondered if we should stop her; clearly the fishing boat was going to be totaled soon. But neither one of us felt capable of stopping a bear in the middle of a tantrum. Emma became more deliberate in her mauling. She deftly hooked one claw into the gap in the engine cowling and ripped off the cover, slinging it a good twenty feet. Finally, having spent the main thrust of her anger, she reached inside the engine with her teeth. She rolled back her lips, baring her teeth, and carefully gathered up the biggest mouthful of wires she could, then yanked hard. We could hear the ripping sound. Her head came away from the engine with wires draped out of the sides of her mouth as if she were eating sedge grass. She shook them to make sure they were extra dead before she dropped them and went in for another bite. I don't know who owned the boat, but the other guide and I groaned aloud in sympathy as we realized the engine was probably destroyed. Finally, Emma walked off into the woods with a noticeable swagger, as if she knew she had gotten even.

All that summer, Emma was a very prevalent character in the cove. Whenever we saw Baylee and her cubs, Emma was not far behind. Over time, Emma started courting the Baylee family. She would try to get close, but Baylee would chase her off, only to have Emma return again within the hour. Guides and researchers began speculating on this behavior. Getting that close to a mother bear seemed like a dangerous thing for a small bear to do. Baylee was twice her size. Everyone was aware of the intolerant reputation that mother bears have. Baylee did a good job of chasing Emma, biting her ears and flanks. However, despite constant punishment, Emma was singleminded. She would creep close, watching Baylee intently for signs that she should move away. Once in a while, Baylee would take a break from fishing to chase her clear over the ridge.

As the weeks went by, Baylee seemed to give up. Then one afternoon, I pulled into the cove to find Emma nonchalantly hanging out, about ten feet away from Baylee and her family. Emma tried to lure one of the cubs to play with her whenever Baylee wasn't watching. The cubs wanted to play, but Emma wasn't an approved playmate yet. As soon as one would break from the family group to investigate this new toy, Baylee would huff or cuff it back. Still, Emma was coming closer and closer. Some thought Baylee would kill Emma. Some thought Emma would eventually give up. Others said Emma must be retarded and wouldn't last the summer.

Despite all the conjecture on the part of guides, researchers, and guests, Emma slipped into the family one day and shocked us all. Baylee had allowed her to join the family, touching the other bears as they slept on the fishing rocks. When they left, she left, when they came back, she was in the lineup with the cubs. She played with the cubs and shared the fish scraps. The final proof that she had been adopted was the evidence of milk on Emma's snout. She had been nursing with the cubs and she wore her milk mustache like a proud badge.

Now, when guests saw Baylee it meant seeing five bears all fishing, sleeping, and traveling together. This was a special show. Soon the word spread and bear biologists from around the country came to watch. Baylee and Emma developed a relationship that seemed unequaled by other stories of adoptions. Since Emma was larger than the other three cubs, Baylee played with her more. The bond seemed to go beyond mother and cub to what I like to think of as "running mates." And this relationship was to become more intriguing as the seasons unfolded.

Other guides and the Alaska Fish and Game personnel told me that the older bear we called Mona had been a fixture at the cove for years and she had perfected a particular, recognizable fishing style, that of belly flopping off the rocks onto schools of fish. This style was emulated by more than one bear. Notably, Baylee seemed to have this same technique in her fishing repertoire. Biologists say that cubs learn their food-gathering skills and techniques from their mothers, so it did enter my mind that Baylee might be Mona's daughter. If that were true, then Baylee was also welcome to share Mona's fishing spot, as mother bears often let their daughters stay in the area where they were raised. However, a bear's idea of hanging out together is much different than ours. A mile interval between bears might actually seem like togetherness to them.

Mona has a way of moving that is unmistakable. She meanders here and there as if she were being paid by the hour. Details in the landscape can absorb her attention until she forgets where she is going. She can stare at something for a long time with that thousand-yard stare. Many a person watching her has been fooled into thinking she was asleep. When something alarms her, though, Mona can accelerate with the speed of a falling rock from an almost comatose standstill. Sometimes she does things so fast that bear watchers who are looking right at her miss it. The researchers guessed that Mona was somewhere around twenty years old. Since bears are known to live between twenty-five and thirty years, this would put her in her dotage.

I hope Mona lives another twenty years, because she is a marvel that we never get tired of watching. Once, on a warm, T-shirt kind of day, Mona walked out of the brush near my boat and waded into the water until she was just five feet away. She moseyed by, not acknowledging us. As she passed me I suddenly realized why people think bears can't see well. She chose not to glance at the people on the boat, and by not directing her eyes our way, she was being polite. Visual interaction between humans and bears usually means someone has to leave. Mona was doing us a favor. One of the guests wondered if she even saw us. When bears are considerate of human proximity, we assume they have bad eyesight. With their ability to discern smells estimated at forty times better than a dog's, it is improbable that bears walk by people and don't know they are there.

In fact bears seem to like to watch people covertly, and they often do things that don't relate to food gathering in our presence. When there are plenty of salmon to be had without much effort, bears will still enter the water in the cove and move past people in boats at close range.

People who watch bears fish often critique their fishing style. Sometimes a guest will remark that a bear needs lessons when the bear dives unproductively for an hour or so. Inefficient fishing, however, is usually a result of already having eaten enough salmon. There are many possible reasons why a bear would keep going through the motions. It could be that he is maintaining his spot in the lake until he gets hungry again. Maybe he just likes to chase salmon, like human fisherman who keep fishing "catch and release" style after they limit out. Or perhaps bears are judging the fishing expertise of humans when they walk by a boat and glance in to see what kind of equipment they have, how many fish are in the barrel, and what the humans brought for lunch.

Teenage bears seemed to be prevalent during our first year at the lodge. In particular, there were two male bears hanging out to-gether and creating as much mischief as they could. Amy said they had been called Streak and Bebe by the staff the year before. (The researchers named them Hunter and Isaac, but Streak and Bebe suited them better.) Rust's Flying Service in Anchorage has a col-lection of pictures under their glass counter at their flight port. A photo of Streak and Bebe shows one of them holding onto the win-dow sill with his claws at Redoubt Bay's main lodge trying to squish his nose into the glass. The other bear is right behind him ready to follow up on any adventure this might produce. The pictures were taken by my husband Mike and chef Juan Carlos, who were at the lodge alone one afternoon. Mike and Juan Carlos saw the bears climb up onto the log stack under the main window and take turns leaving nose prints and smears. Juan Carlos was baking cookies at the time and figured these two were the real cookie monsters.

Finally, the bears rolled off the logs and continued wrestling on the lawn. Mike and Juan Carlos watched from the windows while the bears played like two roughhousing boys, putting each other in full nelsons and chasing each other around. The ground shook every time one of them was thrown down. When the bears took off down the path toward the dock, Mike and Juan Carlos went out onto the boardwalk to watch them. The bears saw them and were happy to have someone else to play with, so they turned around and galloped back. Juan Carlos was new to bears then, so he turned and walked swiftly back into the lodge. Mike was left alone, although he thought Juan Carlos was still behind him. Mike watched the bears as they approached, hesitated, and started to approach again. Mike didn't know he was on his own, but I had taught him to stand his ground in the presence of bears, so he did. The bears were unsure. Obviously, one of these humans wanted to play chase, but the other one wouldn't play. After several tentative approaches the bears backed off, and Mike made his exit, too. Mike says that being on the same turf with bears, so easily within their reach, is a much more profound experience than watching them "safely" from boats.

Teenage bears are like human teenagers in some ways. They have developed sizable bodies with claws, teeth, and noses that work well. Just out of home school with mom bear, a teenage bear is equipped to feed itself and has learned the manners necessary for survival. With a mind that is not completely developed, a subadult bear still has a strong sense of play from its cub years but hasn't gained wisdom. A three-year-old feels bold and aggressive but also insecure and shy. This can be read in his body language. Teenage bears are masters at giving a combination of submissive and aggressive looks. They lower their heads between their front legs just as an adult bear would do if it were going to charge, but the look doesn't come off as aggressive because the lower whites of the eyes show. This is the expression cubs give when they are being submissive.

It is not uncommon for teenage bears to band together for security and play. They seem to dare each other to do aggressive things for the sake of mischief and fun. Perhaps their theory is that two half-brains make a whole. Teenage bears willingly approach humans and, if allowed, would play with us or smell us, rubbing their heads on us to share our scent. Obviously, this is scary to humans, but teenage bears will also leave us alone if challenged because they are insecure. A firm step or two in their direction is usually enough. While watching a gang of teenage black bears move into Wolverine Cove to eat salmon, I noticed that they kept close track of each other. When a brown bear stepped out in the open, they scurried out of there in a group, with the one last in line trying to climb over his buddy.

Weeks after their encounter with Mike and Juan Carlos, Streak and Bebe were playing war games on the south side of the lake. One would chase and the other would run, and then they would switch things up. One of them went straight up the wall of the cove and found a ledge where he set up an ambush. When they met there, the downhill bear who had been in pursuit was suddenly *being* chased, and off they went again. This went on for days, but one afternoon the two bears changed their game and explored an outhouse together.

The Alaska Fish and Game Department had put an outhouse in the woods on the south side of the lake for fishermen. They didn't have the funds to maintain it, so it was pretty rough. That said, Streak and Bebe found it to be just fine. They wrestled their way in, and the door swung shut. The outhouse was not made to contain two wrestling 350-pound creatures, however, and it looked like an animated Gary Larsen cartoon as it rocked and bulged with bears. I was anchored in a spot where we could see the outhouse clearly. Guests were laughing at the sight and trying to imagine the scene inside. That is, until we saw a fishing boat approach the path leading to the outhouse.

As the boat landed, a woman climbed over the bow and headed up the path. Everyone in my boat was horrified. We yelled, "No", as loud as we could, but we were downwind and she couldn't hear us. Suddenly two furry heads peered around the door, one above the other. They looked absolutely delighted to have someone coming to join their games. The door of the outhouse slammed open, and they bounced down the path toward the woman. Her eyes were cast down because she was watching her footing on the path as she walked. We can only imagine what she thought when she looked up. She ran back to the boat, jumped over the bow, and seemed to fly to the stern to grab her guide by the arms. He looked around, saw the bears, and did the only thing he could do, which was pick up a paddle and head toward the oncoming bears. He whacked the paddle on trees. This had the same effect as a more dominant bear charging and slapping his paws on the ground. Both bears promptly dove off the trail, one on each side, and for a moment, it was quiet. We could see the bushes shaking where they were hiding. We suspected they were doing the bear equivalent of giggling.

There are occasions when being aggressive toward bears is appropriate, such as the outhouse incident with Streak and Bebe, or when being stalked by a predatory bear. And, of course, there are times when that would be the absolute wrong thing to do. A mother brown bear may be easy to chase off sometimes, but then she may decide you are acting predatory or being a brat, like a bad cub. In either case she could give you fatal discipline. A dominant male grizzly that hasn't had to move for anyone for a long, long time wouldn't take kindly to an assertive move, such as a bluff charge, either. Knowing what type of bear you are dealing with is the key. The secret is to learn as much as you can about bears so you can be calm if you meet with one. If you are in a panic, your powers of observation turn inward and you can't process outside information. If you can quietly assess the situation, you can act appropriately.

Getting to know some teenage brown bears solved a mystery for me. In the fall of 2001 I had worked as an alternate historian/naturalist on *The Queen of the West*, a river steamboat on the Columbia River. I had always been fascinated by the bear stories in the Lewis and Clark journals, and there was one story I kept coming back to. Most of the stories started with shooting the bear and the results of interacting with a wounded, but very much alive, bear. One of the exceptions to this pattern happened to Meriwether Lewis. On June 14, 1805, Lewis was wandering by himself in the country scouting ahead for safe upstream passage. He had determined that he might not make it back to camp before dark and decided to kill one of the many buffalo wandering around so he would have something for dinner. He picked out a likely candidate and shot the buffalo accurately with a single shot. He was watching the buffalo die and forgot to reload his gun. What a time for a grizzly to walk up! Lewis writes that the bear was within twenty steps of him before he discovered him, and "in the first moment he drew up his gun to shoot, recollecting in the same instant that she was not loaded."

He was on level ground with no place to hide from this "monster" while he reloaded his gun, so he started to walk "briskly"

away toward a tree three hundred yards away. "I had no sooner
terned myself about but he pitched at me, open mouthed and full
speed." Lewis ran about eighty yards, but the bear gained on him
until he ran into the river waist-deep. He knew the bear would
have to swim to reach him. He turned on the bear at that point,
halting into an aggressive stance with his espontoon (a combination walking stick and weapon) aimed at the bear. The bear had
just arrived at the edge of the water, about twenty feet away. Lewis
describes what happened next:

> I put myself in this attitude of defence he sudonly wheeled
> about as if frightend, declined the combat on such unequal
> grounds, and retreated with quite as great precipitation as he
> had just before pursued me. as soon as I saw him run off in that
> manner I returned to the shore and chrged my gun, which I
> had stil retained in my hand throughout this curious adventure.
> I saw him run through the level open plain about three miles,
> till he diappeared in the woods on medecine river; during the
> whole of this distance he ran full speed, sometimes appeariong
> to look behind him as if he expected pursuit.

After watching Streak and Bebe operate, I couldn't help but
picture one of them following a lone human across the prairie.
There is evidence that a teenage bear of the time might not have
ever seen a rifle, and could have been young enough not to know
what a human was. The bears in the area were not hungry and a
game of chase is every teenage bear's idea of a good time.

In late summer of 2002, there came a young bear that we unimag-
inatively called Blondie. She had a super-light coat and was very,

very friendly. She was a gorgeous thing; well shaped with healthy, shiny fur. She spent her days sleeping on the ridge above the cove. Whenever there were people watching and not too many other bears, she would come down and pose. She entertained lots of bear viewers and photographers that August.

I was proudly showing off Blondie to guests one afternoon. She posed for us as we snapped pictures. She splashed around and used a dead salmon to comb her hair. Everything she did delighted the guests. Finally, groping around in the "honey hole," she brought up a still-fighting salmon. Using both her front paws, she stuffed it under herself. When it stopped wriggling, she threw it away and caught another one. It occurred to some of us that perhaps she was getting a sexual thrill from this activity, but no one was willing to mention that out loud. A few days later, I had a group who were not so self-conscious. One of the bear watchers said to her, "Blondie, did the battery wear out?" We all started laughing. That is just what it looked like!

Outside of her promiscuous behavior, Blondie was also a people watcher. She seemed to gauge her performances by eyeing the humans' reactions. Late in the season, one of our overnight guests took a kayak after dinner and paddled toward Wolverine Cove. I was a little worried about him as he didn't seem like a very experienced kayaker. Mike and I took a flat boat to the cove to keep an eye on him just in case. Blondie was there ready to pose for this Japanese tourist, and he was so excited that he tipped himself into the water, camera and all.

Wolverine Cove is not very deep, so we knew he wasn't going to drown, but Blondie was so interested to see someone in the water with her that she started to wade out to him. I will never know what her exact intentions were. She was heading that way with her head up and her eyes focused on the man. Maybe she was thinking of helping. The wet guest was splashing around, startled and concerned for his camera. But, we never gave Blondie a chance to be a hero or a playmate. Mike slid the boat in between the bear and the man, and we picked him up out of the water. Blondie gave me a submissive look and headed back to shore.

Before we left for home in September, Mike and I spent an hour looking for previously dropped anchors in the cove. (Most of the summer the water is obscured with glacier silt, and in the fall when it clears you can recover lost items.) Blondie was there as well. There were no other boats, so we noticed right away when two guys with scopes and high-powered rifles cruised into the cove in a Zodiac. No doubt about it, they were bear hunting. We motioned them over to us and we introduced ourselves. We told them that Blondie was a very tame bear and that she was loved by hundreds of people. We explained that we thought they could get a trophy bear up the south fork of Big River, where the big male bears stay. We told them Blondie was a young female and insinuated that it wouldn't be very sporting of them to shoot her. Bear hunting is a fact of life in Alaska; even so, it is hard to think of a bear you know as well as one of your pet dogs being "harvested." The two guys seemed friendly enough and agreeable. They were local hunters (from across the inlet) and I felt that they had understood. We left to go back to the lodge.

Thirty minutes later, I heard shots. I told Mike that they had just shot Blondie, but he thought the shots sounded too far away and tried to reassure me. An hour later we saw them slowly motor out of the cove. Mike speculated that they had gone back to the cove while we were working and not watching. The next day, Juan Carlos and his mother (who was visiting us during this time) took a boat to the south fork where they found the decapitated, de-clawed, and skinned carcass of a bear. Juan Carlos was convinced it was Blondie. Blondie was one of his favorite bears and he knew her well.

I wanted to know for sure what had happened, so Mike and I took a break and headed out in one of the flatboats to talk to the hunters. As we motored toward the east end of the lake we saw their Zodiac coming toward their camp from the south fork. We altered course to intercept them, but as we approached they changed direction. Since our boat was faster, we were able to catch them anyway. When they saw us gaining on them, they slowed so we could come alongside to talk. I swallowed the lump in my throat and, trying to be neutral, asked them about the shots. They told us they had harvested a blond sow in the cove while she was swimming in the water. They related how it had taken them a while to get her to shore and into the Zodiac, but that for our safety, they had taken her far away to skin her. Per-haps they didn't know that shooting a bear while it is swimming is illegal. I called the poaching hotline to report this, but the officer said it would be my word against theirs and I couldn't make it stick, as otherwise the harvest was legal.

The next day some of our last guests of the season arrived, and we were still very upset. Fortunately, the guests were very un-derstanding. There were no bears left in the area for them to see, so I took them tracking. We covered every inch of the shoreline in Wolverine Cove, poling the boat around. I found the marks where the hunters had pulled Blondie toward shore so they could load her into the Zodiac. There were no human tracks on shore for more than a few feet. It was clear that they did, in fact, kill her in the water, probably as she swam out to greet them.

I am sure the two hunters had no idea what a hornet's nest they were stirring up. The hunting regulations were altered before the next season so it was illegal to shoot a grizzly bear within a mile of Wolverine Cove until September 15. This is a very small step in the right direction. Rumor has it that Amy Shapira was so vocal about amending the law that they called it the Shapira law for a while. One of the other professional photographers who loved Blondie made a poignant poster of her for Within the Wild Alaskan Adventures. I wonder if they would have acted differently had they known their actions would result in new restrictions.

It is amazing to me that humans can see the same thing and interpret it so differently. Those hunters talked like they were terrified of bears. We saw Blondie as a bear who was harmless, fun-loving, and easy to be around. Their thinking was so foreign to ours that communication between us was impossible. Even though I know responsible, honorable hunters in both Alaska and Washington, I couldn't understand why Blondie was more valuable to them dead. Trying to think like a hunter, it seems like a young, healthy female bear would be valued for having cubs and populating the area, leaving extra males for harvesting. Since brown bears are not harvested for the meat, wouldn't most hunters want the largest, most impressive skin they could get? The human side of bear/human interactions is baffling. Humans can be just as unpredictable, excitable, and lethal as bears are said to be.

After Blondie was shot, the bears, even the black bears, disappeared. I hoped they were off to find safe denning areas or had found a late food source. As we said good-bye to the last of the guests and closed up the lodge, Mike, Juan Carlos, and I talked of the next season. We would be back, but we already missed the bears we had gotten to know so well. The lake seemed lonely and deserted without them. The birds still sang the verses of nature's song and the wind, and water added the chorus; but without bears it seemed like the bass notes were missing.

We hoped to find the answers to many questions in the coming season. For instance, in August one of the researchers said he had seen Emma urinate forward—not a thing a little girl bear does. As we noticed the first "termination dust" on the peaks, we wondered about Emma. Was she a he? Was she (or he) retarded? Or was Emma the smartest bear that ever lived? Would the rest of Baylee's cubs survive now that Baylee was also feeding a larger and more demanding mouth? Would Emma den with Baylee? Just like watching a prime-time soap opera, we needed to wait until the next summer's episode for more answers and new questions.

Chapter Four

A Bear's World

Redoubt Bay Critical Habitat Area is on the northwest side of Cook Inlet across from the town of Kenai. Much of the land is formed by years of water running off the surrounding peaks and glaciers making a marshy, flat delta that is braided with waterways. These waterways and rivers are shallow and constantly changing, making navigation difficult for humans, which makes it a perfect place for bears and other wildlife.

Even though people have been going to this area for a long time, no major developments, roads, power lines, dams, cell towers, or other signs of civilization have altered the landscape. Overall, the area seems relatively untouched by humans.

Redoubt Bay Lodge is on a historic campsite, but it is a small part of the habitat. Originally, it was a hunting camp that attracted big-game hunters after trophy bears. After a while it wasn't used much, probably when the bear population was on a subsequent wane. Built on a rock, it is five acres of private land amid the state holdings of Redoubt Bay Critical Habitat Area. (It was grand-fathered in when the area was created.) The Dixons acquired the lodge as part of the purchase of Winterlake Lodge. Both lodges had been pioneered by the Branham brothers who brought their big-game hunters from Africa to Alaska. After the brothers aged past the years of active guiding, the family made a package deal of two of the remote lodges. Carl, who wasn't interested in hunting, wasn't sure about acquiring the smaller lodge at Big River Lakes. As it turned out, it was a great place to appreciate the unique beauty of Alaska. The Dixons improved the lodge and grounds over a period of years. Meanwhile they built up a client base of adventure travelers.

The lodge gets its water from the lake and filters it for human use. The cabins have Biolet composting toilets, which preclude the need for septic tanks. The outhouses are treated with natural lime and the facility only uses biodegradable cleaning products. The garbage from feeding and caring for the guests and staff is flown back to Anchorage at a cost of about fifty cents per pound. The staff uses great care in the handling of fuel and oil, and the Dixons are vigilant in protecting the pristine area. The folks from the previous hunting camp burned garbage and buried it in holes, and we fly it out with the other garbage whenever we find it. Although I'm sure the black bears in the area wouldn't mind a messier camp, the other animals seem to enjoy the natural foods that still abound in the area.

Interestingly, each season has been a little different, and the animals we see adapt to whatever environmental changes occur. For instance, the salmon runs are different every year depending on the earth's weather patterns. The life cycle of salmon spans from four to seven years, and a drought in one year might affect the salmon run five years later. If Wolverine Creek is too dry for the fish to make it to their spawning grounds in Wolverine Lake, the spring number of baby salmon (fingerlings) will be small. When they return to spawn at the end of their life cycle, salmon numbers will be down. The abundance or scarcity of salmon directly impacts the behavior of all other wildlife.

A wild salmon run, like the one that happens in Wolverine Cove, is an event that is as exciting to witness as bears are. The creek that connects Big River Lake to Wolverine Lake is a shallow waterway about an eighth of a mile long. Where it drains into the lake, the rocks fan out to create a rocky, brushy delta. Sometimes, after days of rain or in spring when the snow is melting, there is water in the creek and it is easy for a fish to swim up it. The rest of the time it looks impassable. When the creek is relatively dry, visitors to the cove find it hard to believe that a fish could navigate up what looks like just a pile of rocks. Sometimes someone suggests we move some rocks to make it easier for the fish. Humans always want to improve on nature, but salmon are still a mystery. Science hasn't answered enough questions about salmon yet for anyone to improve on their systems.

The salmon mill around in the cove for weeks, avoiding bear claws and fish hooks, and passing by the creek entrance with no noticeable interest. No one knows why, but suddenly the fish decide to challenge the creek en masse. It doesn't seem to matter if it is night, day, raining, sunny, lots of water or none—a mysterious event causes the salmon to make a break for the lake. They throw their long, muscular bodies up the rocks, using whatever little amounts of water are to be found in the trickle of creek coming down.

When the salmon ran, we could watch for hours as fish after fish seemed to want to commit suicide. Some of the guests at the lodge became so interested in watching the fish run that they picked out a particular fish with binoculars and watched its progress. Running comments accompanied the progress of the fish as they made headway, got lost, or swam back down to try again. Bets were made on which ones would make it to the first deep pool to rest.

Once in a while, a fish gets off track and flops off into a section of the rocks where there is no water to expire slowly in the air. Meanwhile, the bears can casually pick out their next snack from an array of salmon spread out like appetizers. When the bears get full, they get picky and might just take one bite. When they have a really full belly, they just eat the brain, which is one of their favorite parts. The effect of this carnage can be seen early in the morning after the salmon have run all night and the bears have fed undisturbed for hours. There is bright orange fish meat draped over the rocks and hanging from the limbs of bushes.

The other animals come by for their share when the bears are sleeping it off. Magpies, seagulls, kingfishers, dippers, mallards, otters, loons, mink, martins, ring-neck ducks, foxes, eagles, mice, voles, and peregrine falcons all feed on the leftovers. If the bears had not had this food orgy, the other animals in the habitat would have had to wait until the salmon had spawned and died their natural death before taking advantage of this very important source of summer protein. The environment would not be as rich or varied, and the nutrients of the dead salmon would not be spread to the surrounding vegetation and trees. Bears have a quick digestive system; hence if you put a whole lot of salmon in one end of the bear, out the other end comes perfect fertilizer. Bears spread berry seeds around and contribute to the health of other plants in many ways. The lush, green habitat of Big River Lakes is due partly to the long days of sunlight, but also to the fertile soil and various nutrients that abound. In just my four years of watching the bears, it is obvious that the whole habitat would be mightily impoverished without them.

The mallard ducks of Wolverine Cove have earned the nickname "killer ducks" because they waddle on shore to snatch choice morsels from between the paws of brown bears. They have even pulled on pieces of fish that are hanging out of a chewing bear's mouth. Occasionally, they will get chased by cubs that want to play, but for the most part, the bears tolerate them. When the little ducklings hatch, mother mallard has twelve or thirteen little ducks following her around the area. The next day there may be fewer ducklings, and finally, as the little ducks reach flying size before fall, there will only be one or two left.

Drama happens in the habitat even when you aren't expecting it. One guest was exclaiming over the cute ducklings when I felt a shadow pass overhead. The guest watched, horrified, as a bald eagle swooped down, grabbed a duckling, and flew with it screaming and writhing off to the nest. The mother duck reared up as if to do battle with the eagle, but she was no match for the speed of flashing talons from above. On the way out of the cove I showed the guests that the baby duck was being fed to another starving baby. With binoculars we could see the small eagles in the nest fighting for the scraps. Although it didn't make up for the trauma of witnessing the murder, it made more sense to the guests after that. If every mallard mother successfully raised her whole brood, the balance might be broken. The natural world tends to make things come out even if left to do so.

The floating bogs around the lake would make a fascinating study; they are interwoven plants whose roots make up a tight-knit floating basket. You can walk on the bogs and feel that they are floating. I found walking on them barefoot was both pleasing to me and less damaging to the plants. Underneath the bog is a mysterious habitat of tunnels used by otters, beavers, fish, and insects. Close to the "real" shoreline of the lake the bog has started to attach itself to the bottom and will become, in time, a new forest. On the outside edges of the bog, where everything is floating, the masses of plants can be torn apart by wind and waves. Sometimes, a piece of bog will break off and float somewhere new, creating another island. Other times the edges will tear apart, like continents separating, creating a channel of clear water that winds back toward where the hills sweep up from the lake. Trumpeter swans, loons, and beavers all make these channels their nurseries to raise young.

The bear trails around the lake weave in and out of the bog. Some of them can be accessed by kayak. By paddling deep into the bog, I was able to examine parts of the bear trail not easily seen any other way. The trail looks like a tunnel in some spots, with a floor that is part swamp, part river. It is also full of downed logs, rocks, and roots, which would make it a "swim, wade, climb, and slime yourself over" kind of hike. One section of bear trail, from Big River Lake to Martin Lake, is used by the lodge because we keep a canoe on Martin Lake for wilderness paddling. This section is a short, very challenging scramble through devil's club, rocks, roots, and slimy trail. To continue on the bear trail around Martin Lake, a person would do best if he were wearing a diver's dry suit, covered from head to toe in Neoprene.

Sitting quietly in a kayak far into one of the bog channels, a person can get a sense of what a bear's world sounds like. There is the soft rustling of the leaves, the splashy sound of a loon preening its feathers, the squeaks of baby magpies finding their voices, and the soft occasional thud of a dragonfly landing with a belly full of mosquitoes. A little farther away there is water splashing down over rocks and the cry of an immature eagle. We can only imagine the rich interlacing of smells that bears experience, but even our inferior noses can catch the smell of wet mud, skunk cabbage, and algae, and once in a while we can smell a bear. Undisturbed, you could float motionless for an hour or so, noticing all the little nuances of things happening in nature time. A bear can crash through this solitude making enough noise to alert everything for miles, or he can choose to move completely silently and unseen, ghosting through thick vegetation without moving a branch. The only way a person can hope to be as quiet is to use a kayak, skimming along without making any splashes. Although bears can swim well and have been seen swimming long distances, bear watching by boat seems like a fair and safe way to see them.

Summer in Alaska is a time of food gathering for bears, but in areas like Redoubt they have plenty and occasionally have time for leisure activities. As far as I could tell, these activities included playing in the mud, playing with sticks, knocking down trees, climbing trees and swinging on thin branches, sleeping in different spots, and watching people and other animals. Any foreign object, such as a piece of red plastic litter, was the subject of play for at least a few minutes. But the environment is also a bear's biggest predator. Bears can drown in fast rapids, break legs on slippery logs, get caught in avalanches of snow or rocks, or get a paw stuck in a collapse of talus, and they can't call 911. A bear that lives for many years has to be a very wise naturalist, knowing where each animal and plant fits into the scheme of things in order to keep out of trouble. There are many species of animals, such as snakes, that cannot live in the harsh winters of Alaska, so an old bear has also learned mountaineering and snow-cave engineering.

Outside the immediate area of the lodge and lake, there is a river system that comes from the surrounding mountains and glaciers. Two widely spaced branches of river come together at the east end of Big River Lake and feed into Big River, which takes the water to Cook Inlet. The southern branch, or the South Fork, originates at the base of Double Glacier nearer to Redoubt Volcano. The South Fork is a cold, braided shallow river that is full of spawning fish in the later half of the summer. With a jet motor, a boat can travel a good distance up the South Fork. The glacier silt that churns in the main lake for most of the summer travels from the glacier via this waterway. The banks of glacier silt along the South Fork hold some of the most perfect, and largest, bear tracks.

The North Fork comes around the lake from the other side, fed by high mountain lakes and glaciers in the Lake Clark Pass area. The mouth of this fork as it blends with Big River is full of shallow waterways that harbor spots of quicksand. People flying in and out of the area by plane frequently see bears splashing after fish in these unnavigable channels. The wide river plain as seen from the air is extremely difficult to get to. I suspect that the wolves we hear occasionally at the lodge live in this remote valley.

Many of our visitors from around the world appreciate Redoubt Bay Critical Habitat Area as something increasingly rare in the world. Our guests wonder if Alaskans know what a valuable and vanishing resource they have. They find it hard to believe that hunting and fishing are not more controlled in Alaska, not just at Big River Lakes, but everywhere they visit. In the big picture there aren't many places where bears and fish can still maintain a healthy balance. Even though Alaska is huge with wide-open spaces, perhaps we should listen to them.

Chapter Five

Summer 2003

The 2003 summer season at Redoubt Bay Lodge started a bit earlier than the previous year, since we were able to get to the lodge around May 16. Our first guests (who arrived shortly after we did) saw a black bear up on the hill across the lake, and then we didn't spot any for days. We were most anxious to set our eyes on some familiar brown bear faces, like the Baylee family, to see if they had made it through the winter. We suspected that Baylee had denned with Emma and the three cubs, but we wanted to know for sure.

Finally, as we finished our preparations and training new staff, bears started coming into the yard at the lodge. It is helpful if the bears come to us so the new guides can get firsthand experience being with them on the same turf. One of the first things I teach the guides is how to use pepper spray—and then I teach them not to need it. I want them to be close to bears so they can get used to it and learn to be cool. Even though we very rarely use pepper spray (twice in four summers), it's a comfort to have it handy.

I also teach body movements that guides can use as soon as they are comfortable enough in the presence of bears. For instance, turning your head sideways slowly and calmly means, "I don't want to fight. How boring. I can't be bothered," or something close to that. I have noticed bears behaving like this with each other and have had occasion to try it myself. In fact I remember doing it accidentally with the grizzly I encountered in Washington State. Every time I have tried it since, the bear shows me the same attitude, and we part peacefully. There is a catch to this, though. In order for this body language to be effective, you have to adopt a certain attitude. If your knees are knocking together and sweat is pouring down your forehead, it is hard to act casual. Certainly, having pepper spray, or a nearby escape, helps boost your confidence level.

One of the most instructive things that happened to us early in the 2003 season was being charged by a male bear. This hefty old black bear had been coming around, flustering the winter caretaker. He was bigger than the caretaker and had decided to walk along the same paths the caretaker used when he did his chores. One afternoon shortly after the summer staff arrived, the bear came down the path from the hillside cabin, as was his habit, sauntering through "his" lawn. Used to seeing only one person there, he was shocked to find four of us on the porch watching him. I think he felt a bit cornered and certainly his "manhood" was in question. He swung his head ponderously, checking us out from the corner of his eye. Then in a flash, he lunged about ten steps toward us and slammed down one front paw, shaking the ground. After a slight pause, as if for effect, he looked right at us. Simultaneously, we all slowly and calmly turned our heads to the side. He did the same and then exited stage right, nonchalantly, with his personal dignity intact.

When the bear hurtled in our direction his eyes stayed locked on us. As I watched, his intense glare seemed to open a little wider; it was as if we surprised him by not behaving as he had expected. In watching bears react to charges from other bears, I have noticed that a nonflinching bear is intimidating to the charging one. Guests at the lodge tell me this is easier said than done, and I am sure it is, but when a bear is charging you, you don't have many options or a lot of time. Unlike dogs that have attacked me in the past, it looked to me as if the bear was thinking during the charge and decided to stop short. It was a priceless experience.

It didn't take long for the whole Baylee family of five, including the apparently now adopted Emma, to show up at the lodge. We were so happy to see her and all four cubs that we just watched her for a long while. The bears settled on the lawn for a nap just below the main lodge. There is nothing that changes your attitude about bears faster than having to walk around sleeping grizzly bears to get your work done! Baylee took a liking to one of our red canoes that we stored upside-down on the lawn. She positioned herself with all her mammary glands against the canoe and went to sleep. We speculated that four hungry nursing cubs would make her sore and tender, and that uninterrupted sleep was precious to her. Later, we observed her wading into the cool waters of the lake near Wolverine Cove, lowering herself into the water as if easing a pain. She would sit there, safe from nursing mouths, while her cubs played on shore.

While our first overnight guests (a great couple from England) were there, the Baylee family came into the yard as usual, but things quickly changed when Emma looked in the window of the Lakeside cabin. She put her front paws on the logs stacked on the side of the cabin so she could peek in. Suddenly she started making woofing and blowing noises. Baylee ran to her aid and looked in the window as well. Soon, both of them were agitated, which upset the other three cubs. Then all five bears were running around the cabin and peering in the windows. Finally, Baylee looked into another window and started to bat it with her massive paw. At this point I knew I needed to intercede before she broke a window, which might hurt her and scare her more, not to mention the potential damage she could do if she panicked.

I walked down the path toward Baylee. Our guests couldn't believe that I would walk toward a perturbed mother bear, but I didn't give the danger much thought; I was used to Baylee and had reason to believe she'd recognize me. I approached until she acknowledged me with a glance. She watched me for a moment as I talked softly and slowly. It probably would have been just as effective for me to pretend to graze, which is what bears do when they want to exhibit nonchalance. Humans always approach a potential crisis with words, though, even if it is really silly to talk to a bear about the weather. It wasn't my nonsense words, but the cadence in which they were delivered that made Baylee breathe easier. She is much more talented than I am in reading body language, and I was flattered that she trusted my effort to show her there was no threat. She sat down, looked around, then "huffed," calling her cubs. One by one they came to sit with her, gathering their composure. After this pause, she headed the family out to the trail around the lake by way of the dock.

When they were gone, I looked in the window to see what had upset them so much. Peering through their smears on the glass I saw myself in a mirror hanging on the far wall. They must have thought there was another bear in the cabin. To keep this from happening again, we put cardboard up over the windows.

Every year when the bears come back to fish it is difficult to recognize the individuals from the year before. They often have remnants of their winter fur, which can be a different color from their summer coats. They have lost hundreds of pounds and may have new wounds or markings. However, it was easy to identify Mona, even though she had three new cubs with her. If ever there was a mother who appeared to be on Valium, it was Mona. She was first seen at Fisher Falls, the waterfall that connects Big River Lake to Fisher Lake. Her three new cubs were dark little fur balls that looked like they'd been used to clean a stovepipe. They were all over Mona, under her, peeping out from behind her legs in a neverending tangle. Mona didn't seem to notice.

Soon after that first sighting, Mona brought two cubs to Wolverine Cove. She had lost one. Speculation on what had happened to the cub ranged from infanticide by a dominant bear to falling down the waterfall. We will never know what happened. Brown bear cubs have a low rate of survival (only 50 percent) because their environment is so harsh. Mona was also a different type of mother than Baylee. She would spend long periods of time motionless, watching fish in the "honey hole," before she would dive in. Her cubs learned that when she was fishing, they might as well take a nap. The only problem was that sometimes Mona would wander off, apparently forgetting she had cubs. They would wake and she would be gone. The cubs would track her down with their little noses stuck in each one of her paw prints. Something must have happened to make those two remaining cubs pay attention to where their mother was, because they were still with her at the end of the season in September.

Predicting bear activities is like predicting the weather in Alaska.
(If you ask an Alaskan bush pilot what the weather report is, he'll
say he doesn't read fiction.) So, sometimes guests at Redoubt Bay
do not see bears at all. Both the guides and guests are disappointed
if this happens. We have worked hard on our natural history program to make it informative and interesting enough to fill in the
few days when the bears are absent for one reason or another. Our
alternate plan includes a tour of the whole lake, walking on the
floating bog, tracking, and pointing out lots of other wildlife.

Susan James (one of the guides and a longtime friend) and I
wanted to know why some groups of guests were "lucky" and others
weren't. It was a hot afternoon and Susan's boat was anchored a
little distance from mine. We had been waiting for a wild bear
appearance for two hours. Her guests, and mine, were starting to
get frustrated. As they paced the deck they would look at their
watches, roll up on their toes, scan the woods, and then give me
a dirty look. Susan's boat had eight people standing on the bow
looking intently at the woods. They reminded me of something
and I was trying to think what it was when Susan called me on the
radio. "What should we do?" she asked. We were both wondering
if we should resort to the lake tour instead of waiting for bears.
Then it hit me. Her guests looked like predators. They looked like
they wanted to *eat* bears. I answered her that maybe we could get
everyone to sit down and relax. So we both asked, as politely as we
could, for our guests to take a seat and be patient. They did, not
all willingly I might add, and the result was astounding. Within
minutes two teenage bears came out of the thick brush and
started nosing around for fish scraps in the rocks. Needless to say,
our passengers were very pleased.

Susan and I discussed this at length that evening. We thought we may have hit on something useful and decided to do an experiment. During long waits for bear sightings at the cove, we started asking people to adjust their attitudes. One man asked me how, if you have never had patience in your life, you could suddenly get some. I thought about it for a moment and then whispered to him "practice." To his credit, he did practice patience and was rewarded within the hour when the Baylee family came out to fish. Most of the time when we could get folks to relax and enjoy themselves, the bears in the area would feel much more inclined to show up. Once, I took a group of my guests on shore near the "eagle tree" to show them what the lake looks like to a bear. We stooped low so we could go up the bear trail and penetrate into the brush ten feet from the lake shore. There were bear tracks and sign all over. When I found a handy log, I asked them to sit down and look at the lake. We could see out of the dense vegetation perfectly, but a passing boat couldn't see nine people lurking close to the lake shore. I explained that bears decide to show themselves based on what they perceive from their hiding spots.

A week later, Susan and I put our theory to the ultimate test. We each had a boat full of executives from a large corporation. These men lived very busy lives and were used to asking for something and getting it. They were not prepared for disappointment in any situation. They seemed to think it was our fault when the bears didn't show up on time for them. The men began pacing, consulting their watches, and giving us dirty looks, and even went so far as to make pointed remarks about the obviously remiss guides. Susan and I talked quietly on the radio and devised a plan. We asked our guests to take off their shoes. This was met with disbelief and resistance, but we insisted; and eventually they all sat down. As they joked about foot odor and holey socks, they started removing their shoes. This activity took their attention off the woods and made them lighten up. They were no longer focused intently on where they thought the bears should appear. Within fifteen minutes, the bears showed up and they forgot all about their previous disappointment.

Mike didn't get to spend as much time watching bears as the rest of the staff because he was so involved in running the lodge. When he did get to see bears, it was usually up close and personal. On July 16, the day before his birthday, he had one of those experiences. We were sitting on the front steps of the lodge between breakfast and the arrival of the 9:00 a.m. plane when the Baylee family came strolling through the lodge campus. One of the cubs (we think it may have been the one we would later call James) walked up the boardwalk near us. Baylee was about fifteen feet away on the other side of the cub, calmly grazing on cow parsnip. The cub looked like he was just going to pass us by, following Baylee. At the last second, though, curiosity got the better of him and he stopped right in front of Mike. Being careful not to look Mike or me in the eyes, he stretched his nose out and laid it gently on Mike's clasped, relaxed hands. The cub gave a long, deep intake sniff and then glanced submissively at me. I was worried that encouraging this behavior wouldn't be good for the bear's safety, so I gave him a somewhat stern, direct look and told him that was enough. He backed off and joined Baylee and the other cubs and they ambled out of the yard, grazing their way toward the floating bog. Amazingly, Baylee seemed totally unconcerned about the whole affair. She did glance at Mike after the cub touched him but went right back to chewing grass. Aside from getting a little grizzly snot on his hands, Mike felt that his experience was a very special birthday present.

Emma kept getting bigger as the summer went on. It was funny to see this big bear playing and nursing with Baylee's cubs. It became even more interesting when we again took up the debate about whether Emma was a he or a she. Eventually, as all teenage bears do, Emma discovered *his* sexuality and earned the name Emmett. But unlike other bears who may discover this in solitude, Emmett was very comfortable being at the cove with lots of people watching him. Most people look at a grizzly bear paw and picture the havoc those big appendages can cause with their claws of razor-sharp strength. Watching Emmett gently titillate himself was a revelation. Bears can use their paws for delicate tasks. Similarities between Emmett and teenage boys became rather embarrassing for some of the guests. In fact, when our guests watched a bear engaging in any activity they perceived as humanlike it surprised them. Many were amazed that we could even tell individual bears apart.

Emmett narrowed the gap of bear/human understanding during the years he visited Wolverine Cove. We used to joke that he probably rode to school in a small yellow bus. Then, on the other hand, his survival strategy was ingenious. Here he was being completely protected during his teenage years by a full-grown mother bear that provided him with playmates and security, and supplemented his diet with rich milk. Did Emmett plan this all out? Or, was he feeble-minded and really didn't know any better? Of all the bears we got to know, Emmett always left us wanting to learn more.

Then Emmett was injured, and we thought he was going to die. He had gotten too close to one of the other mother bears, and she had chased him out of the cove. When he came back he was only using three legs and had a huge wound on his left hindquarter, which was bleeding and looking very ugly. Then he disappeared. We would see the Baylee family, but Emmett wasn't with them. For three days we wondered about him and finally decided that he wasn't going to make it back. No one wanted to talk about the big empty space in our world that would result. Sadness prevailed, and the guides didn't even mention Emmett's existence to guests because it was too painful to talk about.

Then, in the usual Emmett manner, he surprised us. He came back on the fourth day looking skinny and weak. He was still using only three legs, moving stiffly and limping badly. He got in the water and soaked. Then, dripping wet, he went part of the way up the muddy bank on the right side of the cove and started digging with his uninjured paws. He dug a huge hole in the ground and sat in it. He moved from the hole to the water and back again several times until he had a bear-sized mud puddle. With an audible groan he wiggled himself down in the hole, then used his paws to pack mud all over his hindquarters. When he was satisfied with the mud pack, he found a resting spot for his head and went to sleep. Within a week, Emmett was running around with the Baylee family as if nothing had happened. Within three weeks, there was no sign of his wound.

By August Emmett was as tall as Baylee. He didn't have the mass of muscle that Baylee had, but his bones had grown long and his head was massive. When they "play fought" it was starting to look dangerous. But Emmett was gentle, even with the much smaller two-year-old bears that were his adopted siblings. Emmett's favorite activity was play fighting, and perhaps being part of the group was more important to him than anything.

TOP: *Baylee takes a break from her busy fishing day.*
BOTTOM: *A bear contemplates the grass under a brilliant blue sky.*

TOP LEFT: *Red fox are prevalent in the area around Wolverine Cove.*
TOP RIGHT: *The "cuddly" cubs are never far from their mothers, who though occupied with fishing are also teaching their offspring critical survival tactics.*
BOTTOM: *Emmett tries to walk through a tree.*

BOTH PHOTOS ABOVE: *Streak and Bebe, two teenage bears, test each other in the waters of Wolverine Cove.*

TOP LEFT: *Biologists observe the bears from inside lookouts.*
TOP RIGHT: *Fisher Falls.*
BOTTOM: *The bear called Amy faces off with a black bear; both exhibit classic*

TOP: *An abandoned first-year cub takes a salmon nearly as big as he is.*
MIDDLE: *Baylee's three cubs sunning on a rock. Baylee is nearby.*
BOTTOM: *It's easy to understand how an observer might interpret this as an affectionate moment between Baylee and one of her cubs.*

TOP: *One of Baylee's yearling cubs learning to fish under mom's watchful eye.*
MIDDLE: *The bears around Redoubt Bay are so habituated that Mona nurses her cubs in plain sight.*
BOTTOM: *The bear James loved to take apart beaver dams such as this one.*

TOP: *Bears often exhibit highly individual fishing techniques. Baylee dives for a likely looking salmon.*

BOTTOM: *The bear called Amy with a freshly caught fish.*

TOP LEFT: *Photographer Amy Shapira and Linda Hunter's husband, Mike McHugh.*
TOP RIGHT: *Linda Jo Hunter.*
BOTTOM: *Redoubt Bay Lodge.*

Our collective image of a dominant male bear is a massive animal standing on a mountain, wisely surveying his kingdom in a majestic, solitary pose. You can see that bear on the cover of many hunting magazines. But Emmett could blow these preconceived notions right out of the water. Yes, he was big and beautiful, but whenever he got separated from Baylee, he would moan loud enough for us to wonder if he had another wound. Then, when reunited with Baylee, he would nose her side until she let him nurse. I cannot erase the image of Emmett, the lanky four-year-old, cuddled up to Baylee licking rich cream off his snout. If only we could ask Baylee why she adopted Emmett.

It might be easy to understand why Emmett would choose to be adopted, but what possible motivation could Baylee have? In a classic example of anthropomorphizing, we could say that Baylee loves Emmett. Is it possible for us to believe that bears could experience love, when less than a hundred years ago most people thought that animals didn't even feel physical pain?

Wolverine Cove made the news several times in 2003. The use of the cove by fishing guide services and bear watchers had reached a saturation point, so there were questions about new laws to keep these groups happy. The response by the Alaska Department of Fish and Game was to form a "user group committee" and allow the various groups to come to an agreement on how to proceed. This was called the Wolverine Cove Management Committee and was made up of the people who worked in the guide, lodge, and tourist trade, as well as other private parties. The group devised a set of behavior guidelines and recommendations to keep things orderly in the cove. But, as can be expected when people have different agendas, this was not without conflict. Fortunately, most of the people who use the cove come with professional guides who work with each other every day and who get along as a matter of necessity. There is a marked difference in the activities of people who come to Wolverine Cove primarily to fish and those who come for the specific purpose of watching bears. Fishermen need to be close to the head of Wolverine Creek, or the "honey hole," in order to be successful or to "limit out." As a result, often the bear viewers have the fishing boats between them and the bears they want to watch.

The differences between the attitudes, agendas, equipment, and actions of the two main user groups led me to another observation about bears. The fishing guides work hard to fill the expectations of their guests in the limited hours they have. They use big engines and quick boats and have to be aggressive in the fishing lineup. Their guests also want to see bears, so if they spot one on shore while they are coming and going from fishing spots, they zoom in close so their clients can get good photos in the shortest amount of time. The bears sometimes tolerate this behavior, but most of the time they leave, or at least move out of sight until they are alone again.

Redoubt Bay Lodge guides who devote more time to bear watching try to anticipate a bear's route and anchor their boats where one will pass by, allowing the bear to decide how close it will come. This works very well if they are the only boats in the vicinity. Early and late in the season when there aren't other boats, we have experimented with this method and found it to be very effective. Allowing the bear to make the choice to come closer usually results in better photographs and extended viewing time.

Bears also like to swim. On my way out for an afternoon session, we noticed Emmett swimming across the channel leading into Wolverine Cove. Rather than get in his way, I cut the engine and anchored the boat. He altered his course and started swimming toward us. I told my guests if they wanted him to come closer they shouldn't look at him. They all looked toward the inside of the boat and Emmett swam all the way around us before heading off in his intended direction. We watched covertly, aiming cameras in the direction of splashing noises.

An early-morning incident with a black bear reinforced my belief that one of the keys for coexistence with bears is understanding their language. Mike and I were awakened by the sound of ripping material right outside our cabin. We got up to see what was going on and saw a medium-sized black bear shredding boat cushions that he had pulled from the rack. Mike pitched a small rock in its direction. The bear moved on, but only to the front porch of the lodge. There he leapt on top of one of the freezers (full of human food) and started jumping up and down. This bear weighed at least 350 pounds, so when Mike and I came around the corner, we knew we had only minutes before the bear popped the hinges and the freezer opened. The result would not be good for any of us, as the bears around the lodge have never gotten any human food, as far as we know. We tried the rock trick again, bouncing a stone noisily off the freezer. The bear glanced up with a look that could have been interpreted as "Whatever." I put my hand on Mike's arm and said, "Let me try something."

With the safety off the pepper spray in my left hand, I charged the bear, trying to look just like the big male that had charged us at the beginning of the season. I ran forward and stamped my foot down, and at the same time I slapped my right hand on my thigh. I gave the bear a direct stare. He gulped and looked at me for a second before he flew off the freezer, hitting the deck stairs midway down. He was peeing on himself as he ran into the woods. He didn't come back. Up until that moment I never knew I was so fierce! Mike assures me I am not, so all I can think of is that I had finally done something the bear understood.

Some of the other staff, including Chad Fischer, who had been the winter caretaker the previous season, said they experienced similar responses in black bear encounters. Chad chased off a mother bear soon after. We had a great run of silver salmon for two weeks that August, and Carl and Kirsten sent a group of guests to us from Riversong Lodge. They also sent some guides from that lodge to do the fishing. They were very successful, and when I came in from my afternoon bear-viewing trip the guest guides had forty-seven beautiful salmon laid out between the boats for pictures. As I made my way up to the lodge I asked them to get that fish off the dock as soon as possible before the bears showed up. They were skeptical. They hadn't seen a bear all day, and I wasn't really *their* boss anyway. Besides, each guest had a digital camera that needed to be filled up with fish pictures, and they were far from finished. The fish were laid out in an artful manner like sardines on an hors d'oeuvre tray and the guests were taking turns posing behind the array. Even though I am not a fisherman, I understand the thrill of gathering food, so I didn't insist and trudged on up to the lodge.

Soon after, I got a frantic radio call and headed back down to help them. As I ran down the steps I could see about ten people on the dock defending the fish by yelling at a mother black bear and her three cubs. They had thrown a broom at her and banged things loudly while she sat patiently nearby. I joined the crowd on the floats in an effort to calm the people and then looked to the bear. She was a beautiful black bear with her three little cubs pressed against her sides. She knew there was enough fish to share, so she was settling in to wait. About this time Chad came down the stairs and sized up the situation. He was close to the bear on the shoreline in a better position than I was to deal with her, so when I gave him the nod he charged the bear with his pepper spray handy. He ran toward her, stopping suddenly about fifteen feet away, and slapped his hand on his thigh. The bear immediately got up and hustled her cubs out of sight. She didn't really leave the area, but stayed out of sight while the guides took the fish out on the lake and cleaned them in deep water. (We clean fish away from the docks so that if a bear finds the scraps the food is not associated with us.) When the plane finally took off with the cleaned fish safely wrapped up in the float compartments, the mother bear gave up hope. There was no one else around when I finally saw her come out of hiding and herd her little family toward more promising food sources somewhere else.

Then, a few days later, one of the pilots who flies our guests in told me he had heard a rumor that we charge bears. Just like everywhere else in the world, Alaska is a small place. I was tempted to tell him we only charge a flat fee, but I knew this was a pretty serious thing. It wouldn't be long before the story had us charging at "king" brown bears. Instead, I said that was an imaginative version of the truth and that we had simply chased some black bears off the lodge property.

In both cases we had taken backup precautions with pepper spray. Guests sometimes asked me what we would do if the pepper spray failed. I had thought of that as well, and kept fire extinguishers handy. I have never had to test using a fire extinguisher, but I would try that before using a gun. In both types of common bear attacks, defensive or predatory, the noise, projection, and substance of a fire extinguisher should quickly change the focus. The dock, boats, lodge, and guest cabins have fire extinguishers placed in handy spots.

As the season moved toward fall, darkness returned to the night sky earlier and we needed flashlights to get to our cabins after work. The bears started moving off toward the high country. The Baylee family was just as close knit near the end of the season, all of them sporting new rolls of fat and moving slowly. There was no doubt that the den they would occupy needed to be huge. With all those fat bodies together it would probably be very warm as well.

Research on bear hibernation has advanced in the last five years. Dr. Lynn Rogers was able to put an infrared video camera in a den and discovered that bears don't sleep all winter. Thousands of people watched a mother black bear in her den via the Internet and e-mailed her activities to the researchers. They concluded that bears sleep an average of twenty hours a day. The rest of the hours they open their eyes, move around, and care for their cubs before settling down for another long nap. Washington State University researchers are hand-raising some grizzly cubs in order to be able to handle them while they are hibernating for a study that may help humans with heart disease. Bears may someday play an important personal role in all our lives.

It was time to close up the lodge and turn it over to the winter caretaker. As always at the end of the season, we wondered about next spring. Normally, mother bears kick the cubs out of the nest early in the spring of their third summer. Would Baylee chase Emmett off as well? Would the four of them band together without Baylee? Would Baylee mate again? What new bears might find Wolverine Cove? With just as many questions as answers to think about during the winter, we wished the bears a good sleep and boarded a floatplane to fly back to civilization.

Chapter Six

Summer 2004

Piles of snow collected at Redoubt Bay Lodge during the winter of 2003 to 2004. George, the winter caretaker, took photographs of drifts over the windows and, in places, as high as the roofs of the cabins. George's pictures showed shoveled paths that were almost tunnels between the cabins. The winter caretaker arrives when the last summer staff leaves in the fall and spends about eight months in isolation. Once a month or so, weather depending, Carl, the lodge owner, charters a plane to bring in food, fuel, and mail. The rest of the time, the caretaker chops wood, keeps a hole open in the lake ice for water, and keeps the buildings safe from harm. That means shoveling lots and lots of snow. The caretaker is also responsible for reporting to the National Weather Service. He takes weather observations on an hourly basis and calls the information in on a satellite phone. Believe it or not, there are perks to his job. It is quiet and beautiful in the Alaska wilderness in winter. Caretakers see wildlife that the summer crew miss, like wolves, foxes, and moose. Nevertheless, when spring comes and the days get longer, caretakers are usually ready to see some people and eat someone else's cooking.

At Redoubt Bay Lodge, like everywhere in Alaska, there is a period of time when travel by small plane is impossible. Planes can land on skis when the ice is hard, but as the ice starts to get soft there is an in-between time when skis are unsafe. To use floats to land, the water must be completely clear of ice. As spring's warm winds start melting the ice, huge hunks break off and spin their way downriver. Alaskans call this "breakup." It can happen quickly, with echoing cracking sounds indicating that the ice is finally moving out, marking the end of winter. In some towns there is an annual betting pool about the day and hour of breakup.

Sometimes folks get stuck in the outback during this in-between time. For example, if you fly out to the bush in April or May and your plane lands on skis, it might be the night the weather changes. It could be days or even weeks before you can be picked up. In the fall, this process reverses when the first layer of ice forms on the water. The planes must wait until the ice can support them on skis before they land again. For locals this is par for the course. Many Alaskans have gotten stuck during both breakup and freeze-up. In the short summer season, the travel industry tries to keep regular schedules to accommodate visitors from around the world who are used to timetables. Even so, nature doesn't always cooperate, and fog or wind can strand visitors for hours, or even days.

Every year when Mike and I journey to Anchorage, we never know whether it will be hours or weeks before we can fly to Redoubt Bay Lodge. We always hope to get an early start, and Carl is usually in daily phone contact with the caretakers of both the lodges owned by Within the Wild Adventure Lodges, trying to co-ordinate supplies, gear transfers, and staff shuffling with the plane scheduling. At the same time, there are usually new summer employees arriving who need rides from the airport and a place to sleep, and have a million questions. The logistics are mind-boggling. The lodges need everything at the start of the season, from pepper to people, and the weather makes it so there is usually a small window of time to get everything flown out and return all the winter stuff on the back flight. The problems of running remote, off the grid lodges are like running a constant expedition up Mt. Everest. As lodge managers we rely on Jim Schmidt, the town expeditor, whom everyone calls Jimbo, to move impossible loads of stuff and get anything from an O-ring for an obscure pump to a new boat. The office staff of Within the Wild not only takes care of all the booking, marketing, and human resources, but they also do the mail for the whole crew and take care of new people who forget things like toothpaste. Along with our company's staff, we also work closely and well with the staff of Rust's Flying Service, whose daily scheduling feats are like playing six or seven games of solitaire on your computer at the same time.

Mike and I were planning on being in Anchorage for a few days when we arrived at 2:00 a.m. and checked into our usual spot. Juan Carlos flew in next, and the three of use were scheduled to leave for the lodge as soon as George pronounced the lake clear of ice. In the meantime, Mike, Juan Carlos, and I went shopping for the lodge. We filled our rental car so full that all three of us had to squeeze into the front seat of a mini compact and race for Rust's Flying service just in time to help load the plane. We were happy to see Jimbo. He greeted us in his usual gruff manner, which we always assumed meant he liked us.

When you pack for four months of work in the Alaskan bush, the result is some pretty big bags that look like you are traveling with your own moose. More often than not, these bags can't follow you right away on a small plane loaded with other necessities. We finally learned to pack a separate small bag with enough stuff for at least a week. After some experience, I would never recommend taking a small plane anywhere without packing a backpack for a few days just in case. Our flight to the lodge took off from Lake Hood loaded down like a pregnant guppy. The DeHavilland Beaver floatplanes are the sky trucks of Alaska; and once airborne, we chugged along watching the mountain scenery scroll by the windows at a steady pace.

Fortunately, George was a meticulous caretaker, and starting the season was easier because he left things clean and organized. We were impressed that there was hot fresh coffee waiting for us, especially since George doesn't drink coffee. We felt we were back home as we moved stored equipment and mice out of our tiny log cabin and settled in.

By the time the ice disappears in the lake, the grass is usually green and the snow gone; however, the dock area was still under a layer of ice. As it melted and moved out of the shadowed cove we realized that one of the bear-viewing boat's pontoon hulls had been crushed by the weight of the winter ice. Unfortunately this meant another task for Carl and Jimbo. They had to find, purchase, and take apart a new boat. Then the parts were flown to the lodge, some of them just barely fitting into a floatplane. We rebuilt the boat on site, with Carl, Jimbo, and other staff pitching in to complete the boat by June 15.

Our first lodge visitors flew in on May 27. It was a cold, wet day and we didn't see any bears. The next day's visitors saw two moose grazing in the vicinity of Fisher Falls. Our summer staff trickled out to the lodge that first week. Mike and I were pleased to have Dr. Steve Stringham join us as a guide for the summer. Dr. Stringham had written a book called *Beauty Within the Beast* about raising black bear cubs, and he had been studying bears for thirty years. He would be a valuable addition to the staff. The rest of our new staff had guiding experience but varying degrees of exposure to bears.

As the season started, it didn't take long to have a personal encounter. As in 2002 the first brown bear we saw was a single teenager wandering the lake looking for stuff to eat. On the morning of June 3, we found the small, scruffy bear eating grass right outside the main lodge. He was careful not to look at any of us in the eyes. There was a large bite mark on his right hindquarter. That afternoon, the bear was mowing down fresh greenery near the dock as the 1:00 p.m. plane came in. The guests and staff watched from the stairway as the bear grazed around the point and out of sight. Because of its relative lack of shyness, I suspected that this teenager was one of Baylee's cubs. This would mean that Baylee had finally had enough of her three cubs and the infamous adopted Emmett and was on her own. No doubt Baylee needed a rest after being with that crew for two and a half years.

By the next day it was apparent we had ourselves a "mascot" bear. When the second group of guests came back to the dock after scouring the whole lake for signs of bears, there was the young grizzly grazing near the dock. So far, the only animals these folks had encountered in Wolverine Cove were two moose swimming across the cove on their way to greener pastures. That evening the mascot bear stayed close to the lodge, chomping noisily on new grass and meandering between the cabins.

One of our youngest and most inexperienced guides, Jeff, got to meet this bear up close and personal the next day. We were working on the dock and we had just decided to head to the lodge. I was on the stairs behind him when we both looked up to see the small grizzly launch himself off the top step at full speed. I stopped in my tracks, trusting the bear to figure it out even though from my view it looked like Jeff was going to be wearing a bear. Luckily, the wild-eyed animal veered in midair, avoiding us by a small margin. The bear landed on the bank beside the stairs, then crashed into the bushes. Jeff went up to the lodge to see what had happened, and I stayed with the bear, talking softly. The animal calmed down and started grazing. When I went back to the lodge and compared notes with Mike, he told me the little bear had been resting in the bushes just out of sight and was startled by staff rolling a cart on the boardwalk to the lodge. Jeff felt he should be the one to pick the name for this grizzly, and dubbed him James Bear. Later, it was shortened to just James.

The bear-viewing season was off to a slow start as it was rainy and cold for the first part of June and the salmon seemed to be late. When the salmon don't come up Big River to gather in Wolverine Cove, the bears we see sporadically check for fish and feed on other things in between. Usually, they disappear near the lowest tides in June, and I suspect they make the journey to the coast to do a bit of clamming on the salt flats. When they notice salmon in the river, they follow them the fifteen miles or so back up to Big River Lake and to Wolverine Cove. It's no surprise that the fish runs are as unpredictable as the weather because the two events are related. Although we aren't sure exactly how they are related, I bet the bears know.

According to my log, we didn't have a gathering of salmon until June 16, so James was the bear that most guests got to see. He spent a good deal of his time at the lodge itself and wandering from bog to bog, often swimming where we could spot him. Mona had been sighted with her two second-year cubs over by Fisher Falls, and the guides reported seeing a bear I figured was four-year-old Emmett. For almost two weeks James was the only bear around. Then, suddenly, the fish gathered and all the bears made an appearance.

Each year, elaborate maneuvering and positioning goes on among the animals to see who gets the prime times and spots for fishing. On June 19 we got to see part of this show. Mona, with her two fuzzy yearling cubs in tow, made her ponderous and slow mosey around to the popular fishing rock. When she settled her ample haunches into her fish-watching position, the two cubs flopped down and promptly went to sleep. They seemed to know Mom was in for a long afternoon of staring at the water. Even if Mona had reappeared for the season with blue fur, you could recognize her by her fishing pose: front paws on the edge of the rock, hunched shoulders, and bowed head. While she was at this, the bear viewers took lots of photos, but after a while they wished out loud that she would do something. It's once-in-a-lifetime opportunity to have an extended close-up view of a mother and her cubs, but I suppose we are used to faster changing images. Nature's pace is still the same as it was before we were here, and it usually moves at about the speed of ice forming. However, my guests were in luck this day.

A large bear with light-colored fur moved into the cove area, above the seemingly oblivious Mona, and settled onto a rock above her. The cubs lazily opened their eyes briefly, then went back to sleep. The blond bear detected Mona and started pacing. As he moved around, I was able to get a good look at him in the binoculars. Darned if it wasn't Emmett! He looked gorgeous. His fur was still long and shiny, and he had filled out to become one finelooking hunk of a bear. But Mona was giving him a heart attack. Everything might have been all right if he had just stayed still, but he insisted on running back and forth like he was trapped or something, and perhaps he was. He was so nervous that he lost his water. At that, Mona got up and shook her shaggy head. We could imagine her saying to herself, "Dang it, it was so peaceful here and now I have to go and chase a bear."

The bear viewers weren't really ready for what happened next. The normally slow, stodgy Mona spun like a bull in a shower of farflung mud and moved up the hill like she was charging a red cape. Nobody could even focus their cameras that fast. The cubs got up too, shook off the sleep, and galloped up the slope in big jumps.

I wasn't able to answer the guest's questions right away because the action was too riveting and fast moving. It looked like Emmett took off for the top of the cliff and Mona was after him, but then she got sidetracked by a cub that had caught up and run ahead of her. When she stopped to discipline the cub, Emmett got away, but the other cub was still after him. Emmett charged the second cub but ran into Mona, who got into the chase again. Then all the bears were in the brush near the top of the ridge. Trees snapped and dust hung over the vegetation as they moved around. We saw glimpses of heads, paws, and other body parts, but couldn't tell which bear was where. Mona chased anything that was running.

Somehow, Emmett got clean away. As suddenly as it had started, everything stopped. We couldn't see any sign of a bear, so

I was listening carefully in case I could hear a bear breathing hard. We waited a few minutes, but it seemed like the bears had been beamed into space. Everyone thought the show was over, but I wanted to wait just a bit longer. Sure enough, in about fifteen minutes, Emmett slid on all four paws down the cliff, entered the lake, and came swimming out near the boat. He showed no sign of his previous stress. He made a brief appearance, doing a few classic Emmett water poses for us, and then continued around the lake nonchalantly. All in a day in the life of a bear, I guess.

Baylee's three smaller cubs, now subadults on their own, had found each other at the cove and decided to hang out. It is not uncommon for bears that are on their own for the first time to band together with their siblings or other bears of the same age for protection and to stay near their home ground despite their mother's best efforts to send them further afield. This threesome seemed to enjoy each other's company and initiated some of the same games they had played as cubs the year before. They would all scatter if they caught sight or scent of Baylee. A mother bear has to be very convincing to get her cubs to leave, and all of them sported tattered ears and holes in their hindquarters as a result of encounters with their insistent mother.

Amy Shapira arrived in late June, just as the fish were starting to appear more regularly. It was still cool and rainy with mornings socked in with fog. Usually, Amy's arrival at the lodge brings sunshine in many ways. Her enthusiasm for her favorite bears is so infectious that our guide work, that of helping people realize what a special thing it is to see wild bears, is cut in half. Every guide wanted Amy on his or her boat, and I had to parcel out the privilege. It seemed fitting that the first bear Amy saw was Baylee. Shortly after, James came around with his sisters. We named one of them Eleanor. The other sister's eyes were set close together. Amy and I had been looking at *Grizzly Seasons*, Charlie Russell's excellent book on the bears of the Kamchatka peninsula, and we commented that the bears there have eyes that appear closer together. Misha was named after them.

It was interesting to see Baylee's offspring interact: Sometimes all three and sometimes just the sisters would fish together. James still wandered on his own from the lodge to the bogs, and back to Wolverine Cove. If he found himself in the cove alone, he would linger and fish, or sometimes just take a nap. One day Emmett was eating a fish on the rocks when James came up the bear path on the south side of the lake. The sisters were stationed on the hill above the right side of the lake sleeping. When James detected Emmett, he turned and ran. Then Emmett did a strange thing. As I explained, mother bears make a huffing sound to communicate with their cubs. Up to this point, I had only heard mother bears and cubs make this sound in the family group. But as Emmett followed James he made the huffing sounds. James stopped on the trail and waited nervously to see who was calling him. Emmett approached, huffing all the while, until their noses touched. After that they were pals and hung out together. Then they gathered up the sisters as well. For a period of weeks, the family formed a group without Baylee.

Baylee found them in the cove together one afternoon and chased them, scattering them like bowling pins. A day or so later, I saw them back together again. For humans, the idea of hanging out together means we are in sight of each other. Watching this small bear gang, I wondered if their idea of being together had larger boundaries. Was is possible that several miles of space meant they were together? Somehow, without telephones or e-mail, they were able to coordinate their cooperative fishing times.

Baylee was able to fish whenever she felt like it. She would come down the creek cracking sticks, and whatever bears were there would exit. She was gaining weight and was looking rather relaxed and sleek, recovering nicely from motherhood. Researchers tell us that bears mate mainly in May and June, so Amy and I hoped that Baylee had been out dating and would have more cubs.

On July 1, Amy, some overnight guests, and I were scouting the lake right after breakfast as the morning planes were delayed by fog. We had motored slowly into Weasel Cove on the west end of the lake and I was getting ready to turn around when Amy spotted a bear moving through thick brush on the bear trail that connects to Wolverine Cove. I coasted the boat as near as the lake depth would allow so we could watch with binoculars. We were shocked at what we saw. We explained to the guests that we had never seen a bear so big, and we'd certainly never seen this one. Moving along in the tall weeds, the head and back of this bear looked as big as a locomotive. Unfortunately, it was too far away to get a picture, and the bear trail disappeared into trees at that point. I was hoping the bear had left clear tracks so I could get a plaster cast and take some measurements. I planned to go back by kayak if I had time.

That afternoon, the fog lifted and some new guests had arrived. At the cove, these guests found Baylee asleep on the rocks. She got up and posed on the rocks for them for a few minutes and then left the cove, moving away into the cover of thick trees. The guides decided to leave the cove as well because we heard via radio that Mona was fishing with her two cubs at Fisher

Falls. Amy and I were in one of the small flat boats and we pulled up anchor. Looking back into the cove we noticed something unusual: There were no boats there. The famous Wolverine Cove was absolutely empty in the middle of the season.

We had a hunch that we should return to enjoy the solitude. We slowly returned and found that Baylee had doubled back, too, and was asleep again, this time face down and spread-eagled over a rock on the left side of the cove. I quietly slipped the anchor over the side; we were quite content to watch one of our favorite bears sleep. Since there were no other boats, I picked a spot about thirty feet from shore on the left side of the cove, a place that leaves the bears' fishing spot open. It was a little closer than I usually go, but Baylee was the only bear there and she looked like she wasn't going to be moving anytime soon. So we settled in, too, making ourselves comfortable and talking softly.

In a little while, we were startled to hear a loud crack of breaking brush echo out of the creek bed. I glanced at Baylee but she hadn't moved. Then, as if a magician had conjured him, the biggest bear we had ever seen was right in front of us. Not more than forty feet away, to be exact. An obvious male, he was magnificent with legs that looked like the trunks of giant palm trees and a hump of muscle behind his head that was as big as a microwave oven. His snout was dilated as he tested the air, and his lips were covered with foam. His long blond hair rippled as he swung his massive head. Amy and I were both holding our breath. I thought he would kill Baylee. Amy, thankfully, thought to grab her camera. She also decided this bear could only be called Bruno.

An anxious glance at Baylee revealed that she was languidly rolling around in a seductive manner, looking quite coy. Bruno dropped his soft, black vacuum cleaner of a nose into what must have been Baylee's tracks. He moved one enormous paw at a time in her direction. When they got close to each other, Baylee was standing with her head tilted down and sideways looking at him out of the top of her eyes. That must have been the right look, because Bruno moved in and they touched noses, then turned together and disappeared up the covered path that goes up the creek toward Wolverine Lake. Amy and I resumed breathing. Whew! Amy asked me what I thought would happen next. I said if he'd asked her what I thought he had, they would be gone about forty-five minutes and then Baylee would probably come back and take a bath. We laughed. Even though I was joking, we stayed right there to enjoy the rare peace and quiet. Before too long, we heard the sound of a bear coming down the creek. To our surprise, it was Baylee. We checked our watches and saw that forty-five minutes had passed. Then, she waded into the water! As you can imagine, we laughed with her for a while. All the way back to the lodge, we speculated how cute her little cubs would be the next year.

One male black bear had a very exciting day in July. He found some girls, two of them, sharing a mango near his path in the woods. A lodge guide, Shirlena, had decided to skip dinner in favor of a hike. She and Missy from Fish and Game hiked up the trail behind the lodge to an overlook that has a great view of the lake. Shirlena had received a large, ripe mango in a care package and had just cut it open for herself and Missy when they heard a snuffling sound behind them. They turned around to see an un-invited black bear intent on sharing. The girls were on the edge of a cliff, which dropped hundreds of feet, and the bear was be-hind and above them, staring.

According to Shirlena, they shouted and threw things at the bear, but he would back off momentarily and then return looking more determined. Both of them had pepper spray, but they would have been spraying uphill and into the wind; so they decided to save their pepper spray for a last resort. They also had radios with them. Shirlena tried to raise the lodge, but at 7:00 p.m. we were in the middle of serving guest dinners and all the radios were in the charger, so we didn't hear them. Then Missy tried her radio and was able to raise Vic at the Fish and Game camp clear across the lake. Vic couldn't raise us either, so he grabbed his weapon and a boat and came speeding in our direction. Our guests that evening will never forget the intent young man who came to the front door of the lodge with a rifle in his hand asking urgently where our trail started. He filled me in and we rushed out to the trailhead and alerted the other guides. Dr. Stringham grabbed his gear and ran up the trail with Vic, the other guides following. The guests left their dinner, and I tried to keep everyone calm and off the trail until the situation could be solved.

Meanwhile, the girls had been dealing with the bear for about forty-five minutes. Shirlena describes the bear's attitude as malicious. He locked eyes on the girls and kept trying to maneuver them closer to the cliff. When Shirlena and Missy would try to slide away from the drop by moving into the brush, the bear would move with them. After what seemed to them like a very long time, they were ecstatic to hear the air horns blasting on the trail below and radio assurances that they would have armed company very soon. The bear was astute enough to realize it too and disappeared in the undergrowth as soon as the rescue party got close.

When I talked over the incident with Shirlena later, her descriptions were of predatory actions on the part of the bear. The bear locked eyes on them and snaked its way closer and closer. In this case you must be very aggressive, use pepper spray, or get help. A predatory bear is evaluating people as it stalks them. When a black bear acts like this, it usually has detected some reason why it might prevail and earn an easy meal. Not having been there, I can only say that they were brave in holding off the bear for so long. Missy threw sticks and threatened the bear, but perhaps their panic also kept the bear close and curious to see what they would drop or if they would give up. Shirlena says she will never eat on a cliff with a good view in bear country again. She felt that the bear understood very well that the two women had no place to go. The bear was named Mango after that.

It was always interesting to me that many bear watchers felt free to attach motives and feelings to the actions of bears they observed. The fact that bears are such characters and have quite a range of expressions and gestures makes it almost impossible not to do so. Guides are often are asked to interpret bear behavior; and we always try to be objective, basing our information on our scope of experience. The danger in interpreting behavior is making observations based on our own feelings or single-factor reasoning. For instance, if a bear pushes down a tree, we might conclude that it was angry. It is equally possible that it was making a strength statement to a bear who left a scent mark on the tree that we can't detect. If we had watched the same bear for a week and he pushed down trees on a regular basis, perhaps we would notice that the trees were rotten and contained insects the bear was eating.

One day as we watched Mona and her cubs fish, Mona caught a big fresh salmon and took it up the bank to consume it. Her cubs followed and proceeded to moan loudly, growl, and carry on, making enough noise to be heard on the other side of the lake. One of my guests said they had poor table manners. Another thoughtful guest said perhaps that is their way of saying grace. After watching all cubs of every mother bear make this kind of noise, researchers have concluded that the mother teaches cubs to be aggressive over food to insure their survival. If we could ask Mona, she might tell us that there isn't any fancy reason, cubs are just brats.

There is no doubt that bears in Wolverine Cove watch people. It would be very interesting to find out what they think of us. On really busy fishing days, such as Father's Day, the bears will stay and watch while ninety fishermen enjoy their beverages and yell back and forth. Are the bears concerned for their fishing spots or just enjoying the party? Mona literally breathes down the neck of one guide who always wears a red hat when he anchors his boat in her spot. Does she like or hate red? Or does she just want to wear the hat? Bears study the habitats and behaviors of each human who enters the cove.

Meanwhile, back at the lodge, Mike was checking in some guests who were staying for a few days, showing them their cabins. The family consisted of several generations, including children. The open space of the lodge lawn is irresistible to kids as it looks comfortable and safe like any large lawn at home. It was always important for us to catch newly arrived young people right off the plane and instill some caution in their demeanor before they went running off in their games and encountered a bear. For instance, one of the special features of the Lakeside cabin is the frequently used bear trail right over its front steps. So, Mike was telling the family to be sure to look out the windows before throwing open the door, because bears might pass through the lodge campus anytime of day or night.

Mike was well into his cautionary speech as they headed back to the main lodge on the path. Just behind him he heard the mother say, "You mean like that one right there?" Mike looked up to see a rather large black bear come around the corner of the main lodge. The bear looked as surprised as Mike was. With the family right behind him and a startled bear in front of him, Mike glanced at the bear's eyes and then turned his head, maintaining a steadfast posture on the trail. The bear gave him the same gesture but didn't leave. Deciding it was imperative to turn the bear around, Mike lowered his head and stared right at the bear. The bear retreated quickly back toward the staff cabins. It was easy for us to convince that group that playing in the yard was only to be done when there was a guide with them.

Almost every day, James entertained our guests with his antics. He discovered the beaver lodges built on the banks of the lake and spent a good deal of time jumping up and down on them and trying to take them apart to reach in with his front right paw. What he was after, or what he got, we weren't able to determine. Dr. Stringham and I took a boat over to a ravaged beaver lodge after James left and tried to find tracks that would explain it. It was possible that he was eating beavers kits but we found no evidence to support that theory. Another explanation was that James simply wanted to wear beaver scent. Beaver castor is a highly odoriferous substance with real staying power.

It has long been a theory of mine, based on years of animal observations, that animals like to wear stinky smells to give themselves more personal power. I first thought of this possibility watching a dog I owned on the beach. She would roll in the stinkiest thing possible every chance she had. Then she would parade her smell around me and other dogs in a proud manner. When I took part in the predator survey in 2000 in Washington State, smell was a big part of the operation. The group established survey sites in the forest consisting of scent attraction, motion sensing cameras, and "track traps" to determine what predators were in the woods. The scent was on a piece of carpet that hung from a tree to broadcast the smell. A camera was mounted to catch a picture of any animal who came to investigate, and a raked-out area of dirt was left to receive tracks. Since I lived closest, I was often the one to change the film, read whatever tracks had been left, and renew the stinky lures. I observed that sites that had been super-saturated with scent had no activity in the way of tracks or exposed film on the camera. At other sites where we had applied small amounts of scent, animals had rubbed on the carpet and tried to take the rug with them. One explanation that made sense was that the powerful scent indicated to animals that there was a very dangerous animal there. Several times, as I rode in and out of the sites with the scent lure containers on my mountain bike, I had interesting encounters with animals. I had a herd of elk following me once, and a beaver who just wouldn't leave me alone.

At Redoubt Bay Lodge I learned more about what it was like to be scent-oriented as opposed to using sight as the main sense. When I smelled a bear, I never believed there was one nearby unless I saw it. Conversely, several times I saw bears looking at me and it seemed they wouldn't believe what I was unless they also got my smell. That is why bears stand up when they see humans—to get our scent. This scent orientation seems to cause some basic misunderstanding between us and animals. We smell differently when we are scared, and animals have no trouble picking that up. Hence, people who have been attacked by animals often maintain that they did all the right things, but perhaps they didn't know how they smelled.

One of Dr. Lynn Rogers's videos shows footage of one of his camera operators, a woman, who put on a strong insect repellent before she went for a close-up shot of a black bear. The bear she was trying to film approached her and then rubbed its head all over her, much to her discomfort. If, in fact, smell is most important to animals, then our communication with them has a long way to go.

After attacking a beaver lodge, James spent time spreading beaver scent mixed with his own on the bear trail around the lake by rubbing his paws on his head then rubbing his head on rocks and trees along the trail. I think this might be the equivalent of sending a spam e-mail to other bears that says, "Hey, this is James, and I am a real bad dude."

James again demonstrated his obsession with smell when I had a woman on my boat wearing a strong, expensive French perfume. He maneuvered downwind of us and was standing facing the boat with his nose in the air in our direction. He looked to me like he was excited and was, in fact, dancing in place, sort of hopping up and down on all four paws. He would glance at me, then pace back and forth and put one paw in the air in our direction. It was unbelievably cute, but I was afraid he had a more intense intention. Finally, he just dove in the water and swam straight toward us. I was amused at this typical James antic, but to play it safer I moved the boat away. Knowing James as I did, I wouldn't have been surprised if he forgot his manners and tried to climb aboard. I could picture him rubbing all over this guest just like the bear that Lynn Rogers filmed. I didn't have the heart to frighten anyone at the time, so we just went bear viewing around a little before we came back to the cove. I waited until the situation had passed before I explained that expensive perfume sometimes uses beaver castor as a stabilizing material and that was one of James's most favorite scents. Guests often tell me that they never thought about what they smelled like before they went bear viewing. Except for trying to smell good to each other, we are usually scent unaware.

According to a number of books about bears, folks tend to believe that bears have good noses and poor eyesight. "Good noses" is probably an understatement, but the bears I know seem to have great eyesight as well. As the summer goes on, the salmon in the lake start to die. Their spent bodies float upside down like pale white commas on the surface of the lake. I often observe bears swimming great distances to gather a dead salmon and take it back to shore to eat. That's why, when I noticed a bear following my kayak from shore, I wondered if she thought the moving white blades were fish. Finally, the bear swam out to me. She came close enough to get a good sniff and I held the paddles still for her so she could be sure they weren't fish. After that I saw bears following guests who used the white paddles.

Gathering these dead salmon seems to require a combination of smell and eyesight for bears. I have noticed that bears even seem to be able to tell when a salmon is about to die. When a fish's expiration date is coming up, it starts swimming erratically. First it swims with a jerky motion, and later it spends time swimming sideways and finally ends up upside down. Somehow, using all their senses, bears will swim a mile or more to harvest one of these helpless fish.

Baylee showed me how observant she could be one day when I was anchored in the cove. She was relaxing in the shade and I thought she was being particularly inattentive. Shows how much I knew. After a while she started watching my boat with more than a passing interest. The guests thought she was posing for them and took lots of pictures. I detected a more intense regard. Meanwhile, other things were happening around the cove so I stopped watching her. All of a sudden, I noticed she was in the water ten feet from the boat and staring at me! She was standing on her hind legs with water up to her chest with her eyes locked on me. I looked away and looked back and she was still there. She didn't look threatening, just intent. Somehow I knew she wanted to come closer. At this point, I had come to trust this bear. I asked the guests to look away from her with me so we all looked at the floor of the boat. I heard Baylee splashing close by and peeked at her just as her nose hit the hull of the boat. After the thud, there was a little splash and she backed up about ten feet. She stopped until I looked at her again, and then she brought the dying fish she had captured under my hull to the surface where I could see it before she went to shore to eat it. I may be wrong, but it seemed like she was asking permission to approach when she stared straight at me. By turning my head away, I granted her that permission. Then, either by design or accident, she showed me what it was that she had wanted.

Some say that at Redoubt Bay we don't get to experience real bear encounters as we are safely in our boats and not on the ground with them. Well, that is true most of the time and for most of our guests. You can't live in bear country, though, without encountering bears when you least expect them.

One morning at 6:45 I dashed out of my cabin to get to the main lodge in time to get a morning shower. Right outside the door, James was waiting. Mike had already gone in to do the first weather observation, so I wasn't expecting a bear to be next to our steps. By the time I noticed him, I was out the door and in a trajectory toward the main lodge. So, I just glanced at him and said, "Good morning, James," as if he were part of the staff. He kicked up his heels and went running off in his funny sort of horse imitation. I thought he had gone, but when I came around the corner, there he was with his head stuck in a wastebasket we keep by the outside hand-washing station.

I spoke to him again and he shook off the wastebasket and looked at me. I stopped. He approached. I stood still as he approached and tried to gauge his intentions. He had a posture that was only half aggressive. His head was lowered, but the whites of his eyes were showing, which is a submissive look that I have seen often on teenage bears. Slowly, I turned my head sideways and stood my ground. He stopped and turned his head slowly sideways, and I thought, "Good, at least we have that established." Head turning seems to mean a nonaggressive intention. Every time I have encountered a bear face to face on the ground I have tried this, and it seems to buy some time. James's head turn was a slow, casual one, like mine. But then he came forward a couple of steps; and I decided that was enough, so I moved toward him. He backed up. I stopped. We did the head turn exchange again. He came forward, I moved toward him, and he backed up. Mike was watching this out the window, and though it seemed to me that we did this dance for a few hours, Mike says it was just a few times.

Finally, James moved off to my right, slightly downhill from me, and then turned so we were facing the same direction. I walked forward and he kept pace beside me, and my overactive imagination pictured him carrying my books to school. At the steps of the main lodge he sat down and watched me go in. I wished that I could have just sat down with him and asked him a bunch of questions. I bet he had some for me, too.

If we gave out bear awards at the end of the season, James would have made a clean sweep in 2004 for the most charismatic, most visible, and funniest bear. One afternoon while guests were waiting for the midday plane to come in, James sauntered out of the surrounding devil's club and proceeded to casually eat his way over to the dock. There were at least eight people watching him. At one juncture he managed to slide within a few feet of one of our guests, who got a terrific mug shot of him. He is peeking out between the railings at the head of the dock with his submissive, aggressive look, just like the one he had used with me.

A week or so later, James came onto the front lawn of the lodge while there were about thirty guests waiting for the afternoon planes to land. It was a sunny and warm afternoon, and James stayed in the strawberry patch for quite a while as pictures were snapped of him from every angle. When he got tired of this game, he walked up toward the guests on the front porch of the lodge. Some of the staff were on the porch and the rest were by the picnic table with other guests. After he checked out the porch with sidelong glances and good, close sniffs, once almost touching Juan Carlos's foot, James padded slowly over to the folks sitting on the lawn. He could have walked past them but chose instead to do something different. He moved toward the path as if he was going to go around, but at the last second he stretched out to smell a guest's foot, lightly resting his snout on the man's sneaker. Dr. Stringham stood up from his position on the grass and moved toward James. The bear glanced up and decided to retreat. Never one to take the easy way, James went gingerly around Dr. Stringham and walked down the boardwalk toward the dock. In ten minutes when the floatplanes arrived, James was out of sight. The guest who had been touched by James was delighted and told us that it was one of the most special moments of his life. James is either a very astute people watcher or is extremely lucky. He always seemed to pick people who appreciated his closeness. His gesture was so reminiscent of the time he touched Mike's hand the year before that it cleared any doubt as to whether James was the same bear.

The James entertainment was hardly done for the year. In the later half of August, berries ripen in the hills and bears forsake salmon for something different. It's almost impossible to figure out when this will happen, but the bears disappear for a week, ten days, or sometimes for the remainder of the season. Because of this, we never know what kind of an experience guests will have. The bears could be gone for days on end, and then one day they show up back at the lake as if nothing has changed. Sometimes when we think the season is over, new guests arrive and get one of the best experiences of the season.

That is exactly what happened to some of our late-season guests in 2004. They were staying with us for a couple days and we worked hard to find bears for them; however, it didn't seem like we could find any bears, black or brown. On their last night at the lodge, I took them to Wolverine Cove after dinner. It was a very cool evening, so we gave up around 9:30 and headed back across the lake toward the lodge. When we were halfway there, I scanned the lawn of the lodge with binoculars and saw something. It looked like an old rug at first, and I thought the staff was doing a cleaning. Then the color was apparent and I realized there was a brown bear lying on the lawn. It was dusk, so no one got a picture of this, but as we got closer, I could see it was James. He was under the clothesline. There was a blue towel hanging above him, and as we watched, he reached a paw up and pulled it down. First he took it in his teeth and shook it; then he sat down and put a paw on it and pulled it with his teeth. Sitting there looking for all the world like a teddy bear, he draped the towel over his head so he couldn't see. He waved his paws around in the air as if he were playing blind man's bluff. Then he walked around in a circle, on his hind legs with his front paws outstretched. He plopped straight down on his back end and moved his head back and forth as if he was peeking out through holes. Then he just tipped over in slow motion, still wearing the towel, and started rolling down the lawn. We were holding our sides laughing, and so were the rest of the staff who were watching him from the front porch. When he got to the bottom of the lawn, he rolled out of the towel and sat up and shook his head as if he was dizzy. He picked up the towel again and threw it in the air, pounced on it, and shredded it a little. Unfortunately, night was falling fast and we couldn't see the rest of his performance, but it sure made our guests' visit worthwhile.

The next morning we hung the towel back on the line. Ten days later, the towel was still hanging there and James came into the yard again. One of the guides was over at Wolverine Cove and his radio wasn't receiving, so we motored over in a boat and got him. He got back in time for the guests to see James do another towel show similar to the first one. It was September and it got dark so quickly that we only saw about half of it and then listened to the rest before James finally moved on. Once again, we put the towel back up. In a day or two it was down on the lawn with a few more shredded parts, but no one saw James that time.

As we left for the season on September 12, James's towel was back on the clothesline, waiting for him. One of the guests had added some strong French perfume as a special present just for James. We hope he wore it well.

Chapter Seven

Summer 2005

Mike and I boarded a floatplane at Rust's Flying Service and headed southwest over Cook Inlet to Redoubt Bay Lodge on May 25, 2005. We were ready to start our fourth season managing the lodge. The caretaker was packed and ready to leave when we arrived, so he flew out on the plane we came in on. And just like that, after big airports, negotiating the bustle and intensity of the city, we were alone in the wilderness.

We had brought some nasty colds to Alaska with us, so Carl kindly shipped us out to the lodge right away to get the spring work started and to avoid infecting anyone else. We'd also have a chance to recover before greeting guests. Over the winter, the caretaker and a couple of other guys who work for Carl had expanded the main lodge. The new part of the building wasn't finished yet, but we sure needed the space. Mike built some stairs at the entry and repaired the boardwalk so it fit the new structure. I spent my days breaking out the summer gear, getting boats ready, and looking for bears.

In the fall we pull the boats out of the water and take everything removable indoors. In the spring, the process is reversed. Spring also means starting up the water system, opening cabins, and cleaning everything. Mike and I loved working in this peace and quiet. Except for us and the wildlife, the area was empty. In the evening, when we could turn off the generator, it was so quiet that we could even hear snow sliding down the avalanche chutes in the mountains around us.

Winter was dripping away in the spring sun. The animals were returning. We saw a pair of trumpeter swans looking for a nest. Loon pairs warbled in early morning and songbirds were starting to appear. The golden crown sparrows sang their singular three-note whistle as they claimed their territories for the summer. Every time I had another boat ready to go and did the test-drive, I went looking for bear tracks by the water's edge. Near Weasel Cove I found some fresh prints, indicating that a bear had just climbed out of the lake. The depressions made by the digits were still full of water and the surrounding vegetation was covered in drops of water from the bear shaking its pelt. Although I missed seeing the bear, I'm sure it saw me. I leaned out of the boat and spread my hand over the track. It was the size of a subadult brown. The toes lined up well above the interdigital pad, as they do on brown bear tracks, and the pad looked healthy with long, intact claws registering well out in front of the print. This tangible sign of a bear nearby gave me a big grin. I wished I had a nose that could pick up the nuances of the bear's smell so I could tell exactly which one it was. When I got back to the lodge, Mike pointed out the tracks on the boardwalk that had appeared when we weren't looking. I suspected that the bear I had just missed at Weasel Cove had beat me back to the lodge. Perhaps it was checking out who else had arrived for the summer season.

The buzz of mosquitoes told us it was truly spring in Alaska. Porcupines were enjoying the secluded grassy area that was created by the elevated floor of the new wing of the lodge. Every evening the "quill cushions" would be grazing around the lawn. The eagle pair was back, and the two birds would swoop close to the lodge in their hunting forays. Mallard pairs swam along the shore like couples holding hands. Black bear tracks were in all the usual places around the staff cabins and outhouses. Moose munched on the new plant life popping up in the floating bogs. The lake was clear in spring, and we could see the little salmon fingerlings that had washed down from the upper lakes with the snowmelt. We were always happy to see the fingerlings as they munched on the mosquito larvae. Even though everyone hates mosquitoes, we wouldn't have salmon without them.

Of course, just like the previous three years, I was anxious to see if all the bears had made it through the fall and winter. I knew I had to be patient. Every season I had to make the adjustment from a fast-paced life to the rhythm of nature, where all things reveal themselves in time. The summer guests get off the floatplanes with the buzz of civilization clinging to them like lint, but they would be happy to know that in spring I'm just as anxious as they are.

When the snow starts to melt and drip into dens, the bears start to stir. They come out of their dens and lie around outside for a while. Their noses work overtime to pick up the news. When they sniff, they can tell if a moose died in an avalanche or if any other bears are out. In fact their powerful noses can probably tell them more than we know about the world via all our Web cams and fancy electronic sensing gear.

Once bears have cleaned up all the frozen meat they can find, they head to the valley floor for "greenup." That's what we call the tender little shoots of plants that come up in places where the snow has just melted. They have 25 percent more nutrition than mature plants. Mother bears teach the cubs to eat these plants by letting them lick their lips as they eat. The "greenup" moves back up the mountains as the snow recedes to higher altitudes. By the time we arrive at the lodge each spring, the bears are probably on their second visit to lower elevations.

I like to think of bear meals in terms of seasons instead of times of day. For them, summer is one long four-course repast. The spring "greenup" would then be the salad course. There's evidence that the bears in the Big River Lakes area head to the coast fifteen miles from the lodge to go clamming at the June full or new moon, when the tides are lowest. I like to think of that as hors d'oeuvres. The bears disappear completely from the areas around the lake, sometimes for days. During this time they are also interested in mating. According to biologists, the mating season for bears is May through June. Although I have seen mating behavior at other times, I believe this is generally true. Perhaps the adult bears are out on the tidal flats flirting and not letting the teenage bears in on the game. I've always imagined a teenage bear sitting alone by the river, thinking the world is unfair, when it spots the first salmon: the main course. This may explain why in all four years we have spotted a single subadult bear around the lake about when we see the first salmon rolling. When enough salmon have traveled into the area to school up in Wolverine Cove at the base of the creek, all the bears come through to start the main course of the summer meal.

About August 15 the berries ripen. This sugary treat must be the dessert course. If you pay attention to the subtle smells you can get a whiff of the sweetness in the mountains, even at the level of the lake. For a bear, this must be an overpowering smell, one that is good enough to make them leave the salmon for a while. Typically, sometime in the latter half of August, the bears disappear for a few days, sometimes as many as ten days. It is a weather-dependent event, like almost everything else in the habitat. Bears return to the main course after dessert, coming back to the lake for late salmon. Fall is the time of hyperphagia, when bears become intent on stuffing themselves for winter. After all, by the time we are stuffing ourselves on Thanksgiving turkey, the bears are fasting in their dens.

In May the cow parsnip and devil's club, which grow over our heads in the summer, are all lying on the ground. The stalks are a dull brown and are softened by being under snow all winter. For a short time, before they revive, you can walk around without a machete. I wanted to take advantage of this time and have a good look at Weasel Hill near the entrance of Weasel Lake. We often take the boats to this spot on our bear-viewing trips because bears are frequently seen there. For one thing, the main bear trail goes over this hill and bears cross at the shallow entrance to the lake made by the short waterway between lakes. On top of the hill is an old campsite used by the original owners of the lodge. The initials of one of the Branham brothers are carved in the bark of one of the larger trees on the knoll. Fittingly, bears have left their signature claw marks on the same tree.

I was interested in examining a series of deep depressions on the hill that are very hard to see in the summertime. When I stepped down into one of them, I was surprised that it was waist deep. The circumference of the hole was about eight feet at the rim, narrowing to a cozy three feet at the base. With the vegetation at full height, a bear could sleep in one of these without detection from any direction. The hill was pockmarked with these depressions. No wonder bears seemed to disappear here while we were watching them. The holey hillside reminded me of some tracks shown to me by Dr. James Halfpenny in a tracking class in Yellowstone National Park. The bears in a place called "bear valley" had historically padded the same trail, putting their paws in the same spots and making a deep ditch of tracks. Near these tracks was a "marking tree" where bears left their claw marks, just like the tree on Weasel Hill. Although there are other possible explanations for these holes, it looked to me as if the bears had used this hill for day beds for hundreds of years, making these deep depressions by sleeping in the same spots. I decided it was too dangerous to take guests to see them, as it would have been a perfect spot to accidentally step on a sleeping brown bear.

On my way back to the boat I noticed some fresh tracks in the flattened vegetation. They were indicated only by a slight color change, drier spots, and broken twigs. At first I thought they were bear tracks. I backtracked, marking each one with stick in the ground. As I scanned a whole a section of tracks, I could see the pattern of the animal's gait. The tracks were in a straight line; very un-bearlike. I finally found a print that gave me more details in softer ground. By spreading my hand across the width I could tell it was almost four inches wide and about five and a half inches long. There were four digits with the two front toes pulled together, which are characteristics of canine tracks. The only animal in the dog family with a track that big is a wolf. We haven't seen wolves at Redoubt Bay in the summer, but I have found their tracks several times, making me wonder how often we have just missed seeing them.

Mike and I worked with many talented guides and house staff while at Redoubt Bay, but in the 2005 season, the chemistry of the staff was outstanding. Since we had returning guides, we were able to develop the natural history program a little further. All of us agreed to work on sense awareness with guests, and in some cases, we were spectacularly successful.

One afternoon, I had eight patient guests with me in the cove. We had been waiting for an hour. Finally, one guest asked me if anything was ever going to happen, and he suggested we go somewhere else. I didn't want to leave because I was pretty sure that a bear was just out of sight. I had seen a tree branch jump up and down where there was no wind. To keep everyone interested, I pointed out a little bird that was working the shoreline. My impatient guest said he hadn't noticed it and wanted to know what it was. I asked him to describe what it was doing. "Break dancing, I think," he finally said. I could tell from his imaginative answer that he was now engaged and content to hang out a little longer. The little bird was dipping its body up and down, but while it was doing that, it was slipping and sliding on the rocks close to the water, spinning and bobbing. Every once in a while, it would make a big hop, landing on another rock, and start in with the same routine. In the middle of a twirl, the bird would dive into the water, come up, and shake its head. Sometimes it would disappear underwater for a few seconds.

The little dance was entertaining, and everyone wanted to know more about the bird. Instead of just giving the bird's common name I asked them what they would call it if they were the first ones to see it. They came up with "dipper duck." Then I told them they were pretty close, as it was an American dipper. If I had given them the name first, they would never have watched it so closely. Our minds trick us. If we label something, we immediately put that thing away and stop focusing on it. In the midst of this conversation, the shy bear who had been watching from the brush suddenly felt comfortable enough to come out. The rest of the afternoon was magical, and more important to me, I had learned a new way to engage guests in their surroundings.

The first bear I saw in 2005 was a black bear walking through the lodge campus on May 30, when Mike and I were still there by ourselves. We also saw a black bear on the trail across the lake that day with binoculars. Our first guests came on June 1, and they got a glimpse of a black bear that afternoon. And so the season officially began. On June 2, we saw a black bear mother with two tiny cubs traversing one of the floating bogs by Fisher Falls. We started seeing the first salmon in Wolverine Cove on June 2 as well.

Because we had seen Baylee leave the cove with Bruno the year before, we were all anxious to know if Baylee would be returning to Wolverine Cove and, most importantly, if she would have first-year cubs. As in the past, the black bears had been around the lodge campus trying to scare the winter caretaker into sharing the last of his food. But when there are suddenly more people at the lodge, they are a little stealthier.

Usually there is one bear that thinks the lodge still belongs to him, and this year was no exception. A big black bear male I called Oscar decided one morning that he was going to own the outhouses. Oscar and I were staring at each other, but there was a planeload of guests on the way, so I was willing him to leave. I made an aggressive step toward him and lowered my head. He got up nervously and started up the hill. Unlike the motherly huffing sound, bears also make a noise that I call blowing. It is sort of a "whooh whooh" of breath. It indicates nervousness, I believe, although I would rather ask a bear what it means to be sure. Oscar was blowing and whomping as he started up the hill. It was then that I remembered I didn't have my pepper spray with me. Either my body language changed or he read my thoughts, and he sat down again and gave me a smug look. With a black bear, who was used to being pushed around by brown bears, this was a touchy juncture.

I walked toward him, stopped, and slapped my thigh, which made a noise like a bear slapping a paw down. "Oscar," I said in as low a voice as I could muster, "You don't scare me, and if I have to go back to the cabin and get the spray, you are outta here!" The bluff worked, and he ran up the hill, ducking under some thick plant growth until he was out of sight. After he left, I examined the outhouses and, sure enough, he had placed his paws high up on them, leaving very fresh muddy bear prints clearly outlined on the doors. Strangely, after the guests arrived a few minutes later and used the outhouses, no one mentioned this to the staff when they came into the lodge to register and hear the orientation. Did they not see them? Or did they believe we put them on the outhouses ourselves in order to be more scenic? Sometimes I am just as puzzled by human behavior as that of any other animal. But, at least I could ask them, so I did. They said they didn't see them, but if they had, they wouldn't have used the outhouses!

During the first week in June we also spotted a very small black bear who spent most of his days way up in the eagle tree, which was a very tall birch with an eagle nest about ten feet from the top. This little guy was probably a teenage bear who was newly separated from his family. Certainly he had adopted a good survival strategy by living as high up as he could.

By June 4 all of the staff had arrived and the first brown bears were sighted near Wolverine Cove. They were two small, female bears that were also using the path around the lake. Their pattern was very like the one that Emma/Emmett had exhibited our first season and that James took up when he was first separated from Baylee. I speculated that these two bears could be third-year cubs that had been with Mona the year before.

We also expected to see James and his siblings at the lake, because male bears usually don't disperse to their own territories until they reach sexual maturity. Female bears may continue to use the feeding spots that their mothers taught them about for their own cubs.

The salmon were early, so there was a healthy run of salmon on June 6. They splashed, squirmed, and flipped their way up Wolverine Creek, leaving the cove to travel to Wolverine Lake where they would spawn. These early salmon had an easy time of it as there was still plenty of water coming down from the lake for them to swim up. I hoped that the sound of salmon slapping on the rocks would call the bears, and the bloody smell of the first salmon killed would go out like a mass e-mail and soon all the bears would come by. Surprisingly, the first salmon we saw killed was by a bald eagle, and the blood scent did bring all kinds of activity to the cove.

The annual bear sorting was about to begin. There were five subadults, or teenagers, on the early salmon run. As far as I could tell, they were Mona's two daughters, who had bite marks on their hindquarters and ears, and all three of Baylee's cubs from 2002. A mother with second-year cubs was there as well. In the spring no matter how well you have known them from prior years, it is very hard to recognize the bears. This is because they are all a different color and weight and they still have part of their winter fur. The only way to figure out which bear is which is to watch their behavior.

The mother and two cubs didn't look familiar to me, as there had been no mother with new cubs the year before, so I thought perhaps we had a new bear on the scene. For a while I thought she was a bear we had called Dove, but when Amy arrived she called this bear "Not-Dove." She had photographed Dove for several years and was sure this was a different bear.

One day, as I watched the subadults take turns fishing, they suddenly scattered. Two scampered out of the cove on the left side and the others scooted up the ridge on the right side. An adult grizzly bear came out of the brush from up the creek and stood on the rocks at the head of the cove. She looked me in the eyes, and even though she was at least two hundred pounds bigger and quite a bit darker than the Baylee I remembered from the year before, I recognized that look. It had to be Baylee! I was very happy to see her, but I was confused; I thought for sure she would have cubs with her. Later that evening I e-mailed Amy that I had seen her, but that she had no cubs. We were both disappointed.

My trips to the cove at this point in the season were usually limited to running people back and forth and fixing boats. Every day that guides went out with guests without me, I grilled them about the bears they saw, waiting for more news of Baylee. Frank and Jeremy, two of our guides, shared digital photos of the bears they saw and we all worked toward positively identifying them. Juan Carlos went looking whenever he could, and he thought he had spotted James. Finally, on an evening trip, Rocky and Jessica (second-season staff) reported seeing two mother grizzlies with cubs, one with second-year cubs and one with first-year cubs. It wasn't until June 24 that I finally got to see Baylee with her two new cubs of the year. I was so happy that I e-mailed Amy immediately.

The next time I saw Baylee and her cubs I realized why I had been so confused. Baylee must have had her cubs with her the first time. They just wouldn't come out. As a matter of fact, these two little cubs were real brats. Whenever Baylee huffed to them, they would do something all right. They would run the other direction.

One afternoon, Baylee and cubs came in to fish from up the creek. Baylee was looking into the water, and the two brats wandered up the steep bank on the right side of the cove, stopping on a ledge where some of the bears go to eat fish in safety. Baylee looked up, and when she noticed where they were, she huffed. They were tentatively moving toward her when she huffed again. Instead of obeying the "come here" command, the cubs turned and ran back up to the ledge. Several times Baylee tried to coax them to her. When they scurried even farther up the hill, she had to go herd them bodily to the beach by pushing them ahead of her. Ah, the joys of motherhood.

As the fish came in, so did the human fishermen. By the middle of June, all the guide services that use the cove were bringing folks in to try for sockeye. James started fishing in the cove between Baylee's visits. When James was first sighted, he still had some of his shaggy winter fur. It looked like he had a huge bump on his back end, just above the tiny bear tail. Some of the guides referred to him as "double butt." When I got a chance to watch him for a while, I had no doubt that this was James. He would swim out in the cove, fishing with his head underwater. He wouldn't get his ears wet unless he saw a concentration of fish. When he ran blindly into a fishing boat, he would stand on the bottom on his hind legs and look into the boat at very close range. James repeatedly came within a few inches of fishermen and bear watchers. Several times I saw fishermen leave their prime spot in line, shaking their heads over close encounters with James. It seemed to me that James thought he had made them all leave and he was proud. James didn't seem to be aggressive in his approach, but if someone had given him a fish I'm sure he would have adapted very quickly. No fishing guide wants a teenage male brown bear slobbering on the rails of his boat, inches from his guests. It is one thing to do bear viewing and photographing up close, and another to smell a bear's fish-breath. Although James's antics were amusing to me because I knew him as a gentle bear, I also knew he might swat at someone who made a startling move right next to him.

There were several sets of black bear cubs in the area. Sorting them out was almost impossible because the mother black bears were quite secretive. They were seen at widely different places on the lake, and came to the cove seldom enough that we didn't get to know them as well as the brown bears. One rather small mother black bear brought her single cub to the cove and put it up a tree on the roosting spot, that place on the ledge where bears went to eat fish in safety. Then she proceeded to ghost in and out of the brush around the cove, finding scraps and avoiding brown bears for a few hours. The cub was very patient, but after four hours it started to cry. No mother showed up. Finally, the cub crawled down, its tiny claws scraping the bark to slow its decent. On the ground, it looked around warily before it scooted into the thick brush up the hill. A while later, the mother came back to check on her cub and it was gone. She sniffed around for a while and then left, going another direction from the one her cub had taken. Whether they were reunited or not remains a mystery, as neither bear was seen again all summer. I would like to believe that she searched the whole hill until she found her little one hiding in the brush. Statistically, cub survival rate is only 50 percent due to the harsh environment in which they are raised.

Black bears have a different personality from brown bears. I attribute much of this to their eating habits. Black bears are truly opportunistic feeders. They will put anything in their mouths to see if it tastes good or gives them nutritional benefit. They lick gasoline and oil, and eat plastic, insulation, and all manner of manufactured materials. If you leave something outdoors, it will inevitably have black bear tooth marks on it. Our brown bears, on the other hand, seem to prefer natural foods. They are the health food nuts, and the black bears are the junk food eaters. I think that you could leave a ham sandwich outside at Redoubt Bay Lodge and the brown bears wouldn't touch it, but a black bear wouldn't think twice before popping it into its mouth. This, however, only holds true in a habitat like Big River Lakes, where there is plenty of natural food for brown bears and the habitat has never been altered by humans. In other spots where brown or grizzly bears live, they need to learn to supplement their health food diet, and in so doing, change their personalities as well.

The other reason black bears are different in the Big River Lake habitat is that they live alongside brown bears. This puts them on edge and makes them lack a sense of humor. They're always worried they are going to be beaten up. Once, I was in a boat fixing an outboard at the entrance to Weasel Lake. I was leaning over the transom, watching the engine cooling water, when I glanced up and noticed a black bear sneaking through the fireweed stalks in my direction. I finished up quickly and started the engine, which fortunately was working better. I watched the bear until he showed me his face and locked his eyes on me. He was padding toward me and entered the water, coming straight for the boat. I watched him, looking directly into his eyes while I kept my hand on the shift lever. When he lifted a paw to bring it down on the edge of the boat, I put the engine in reverse. His paw missed. I backed up and he looked sideways as if he were pretending he hadn't done that. I backed away and took off, realizing I had read about this stalking behavior, but had never seen it. I don't know what he would have done, but boarding the boat was definitely part of his agenda. I suspect that my attitude of leaning over the engine and hanging in the water made him think I was weak, and, ultimately, perhaps edible.

The next time I saw aggressive black bear behavior I was in a pontoon boat with guests at Fisher Cove. We were following the progress of a black bear on shore. In retrospect I was probably too close to the bear, because he suddenly dove off the bank and swam straight for the boat. Without thinking, I moved forward in the boat to meet his advance, and he veered off. This was a bluff charge, and a very gutsy one at that. The bear in the water was two feet below us and he was charging seven people.

If a black bear lives to be a big old male in this area, he has to have a very belligerent attitude. One big male black bear (probably Oscar) proved this to me in Wolverine Cove. I was in a flat boat with a couple of great guests, anchored close in. The female guest told me she was very nervous around bears, so I was being careful to make her feel safe. When I saw this big male black bear enter the cove near the top of the ridge, I reached into my dry bag for my pepper spray and set it on the seat next to me. Something about his walk and posture made me take this bear seriously. He picked his way down the slope, stopping frequently to stare malevolently at everything around him. There were a few other boats around, but none were in front of us. Finally, the bear was straddling the rocks at the head of the cove, about fifty yards away. His wide stance and dour look suggested he was feeling quite ornery. Then my guest sneezed. When she looked up, the bear was looking directly into her eyes. Eyes locked, the big bear started moving toward her steadily, silent and intent. I was sitting just behind her, watching this drama as I flicked off the safety on my pepper spray.

The bear entered the water and started to wade toward us, keeping his eyes glued to my guest. When he got close enough for a good pepper spray into the snout, I leaned around her and caught his attention with my voice, "Don't you even think about it." He checked me out and then turned his big head sideways nonchalantly. I set the pepper spray back down. He moved off sideways, ponderously, with sense of dignity and personal power, just as I recommend people do. I hadn't realized I was so scary, but my meaning was clear and bears are good at reading intentions. I believe in giving a warning before using that awful pepper spray. However, that means you have to use body language that is not a bluff. I wouldn't have hesitated if the bear continued toward us. In this case, it was probably a good thing I was the only one who noticed the storm brewing on this bear's brow. Had my guest acted afraid, screamed, or scrambled away, it could have been a tough encounter for all of us, capped off with a huge dose of pepper spray.

We did end up spraying a bear at the lodge, though. Throughout the season we had a visitor that Mike named Beavis. We couldn't call him Butthead. That is politically incorrect. Since we called him Beavis, everyone made the connection anyway. Beavis was a young adult male black bear. I'm sure of this because Beavis once sat down, spread his legs, and showed me all his equipment (whether by accident or design I will never know). Beavis was at the lodge almost every day, but most people didn't see him. In spring when we arrived, the vegetation around the lodge was about ankle high in places where the lawn wasn't groomed. By July, this same vegetation, composed of cow parsnip, devil's club, and assorted bushes, was over our heads. Beavis slept in the tall cow parsnip plants and other vegetation just ten feet from our board-walk paths. He was very used to all of us, the sound of our voices, footsteps, and smells, so he thought it was okay for him to hang out since we never chased him off. It was probably confusing that we never paid attention to him unless we saw him. When we did see Beavis, he was usually doing something we didn't welcome, like peering into the outhouses. Once between the midday plane changeovers, Beavis walked out of the bushes and sat down by the outhouses. Two guides tried to move him off, but since he had been there for a while, he just couldn't understand what all the excitement was about. He wouldn't move no matter what they did. Finally, I walked up and succeeded in bluff-charging him to get him to reenter the bushes. He walked up the trail ten feet, sat down, spread his legs, and gave me a pleading look. He seemed so pathetic that I gave up.

All the guests on the property walked up to look at him, but that didn't bother him a bit. He just sat there exposing himself and looking dopey. It wasn't until later, after I had taken time to track him, that I realized he was in the habit of lounging in our area. No wonder he didn't see any reason to leave! We never told our guests when we walked them up from the plane that Beavis was in the bushes watching them. Many folks come off the plane with mixed feelings about bears, and walking right past one would be a bit much for them.

I was out with guests on the lake when Mike finally had to spray poor Beavis with pepper spray, but Melissa and Jeremy, two of our guides, managed to get a great video of the whole thing. Beavis decided he didn't need to stay hidden and was wandering around biting things. He took a big bite out of our plastic hand-washing station and proceeded to look in all the windows and mouth everything he could find. Mike went out to reason with him, pepper spray in hand. Jeremy tried to take his picture, but Beavis wanted to *use* the camera, not be its subject. When Jeremy retreated to his cabin, Beavis banged on the door. Mike and Matt, our second chef, came up the path to the out-house and Beavis approached them, occasionally glancing side-ways in a half-hearted attempt to look submissive. Matt and Mike gave him warning body language by stepping forward pur-posefully, but he still approached. Finally, when Beavis was about five feet away, Mike gave him a blast of pepper spray. The video shows immediate results. The bear spins and tears up the hill, throwing dirt. On the film you can hear Mike mutter, "I hate to do that."

Beavis stayed away for about an hour. Then we noticed he was asleep in the front yard. Melissa went out to film him some more, and Jeremy went along as moral support. Beavis gave them a great show, standing on his hind legs and licking the windows of the Lakeside guest cabin. I ran him off again, this time without need-ing the spray, and eventually we came to a compromise. He could stay, he just needed to stay out of sight.

He did stay out of sight fairly well, but it seemed as if he couldn't help his propensity for wanting to be close to people. We had a group of five guests who were willing to try everything. One day they took off in kayaks, heading for Weasel Lake. Beavis was around the dock while they were launching, but he was being good and staying out of sight. But when all those paddles started going, he had to join in. Beavis stood up on his hind legs on the edge of the bog very near one of the guests. The guest wasn't used to kayak paddles and tried to back up in a hurry, burying the paddle and neatly tipping himself over right in front of Beavis. Mike and I were in the generator shed and the guides were on the dock. We all started for the boats to help the guest, but he managed to maneuver himself and boat to the dock and asked that we not help him. He went up to change his clothes and then went out kayaking again. I caught the look on Beavis's face as the kayak went over, and I think he was just as startled as the guest. He used this moment of confusion to leave the dock area and swim around the corner out of sight.

The two female bears that we had decided were Mona's cubs needed names. One of the guides, Jessica, suggested we call them Donna and Amy, after Amy Shapira and her friend Donna, who often came with Amy to the lodge. I agreed to this, knowing that it could be a mixed blessing. Ever since I had witnessed the hunting of Blondie, I was afraid to get too attached to the bears. But these two were inseparable and these names seemed so appropriate. Donna and Amy hated (or loved) the outhouse put near Wolverine Cove by the Fish and Game Department. They often slept on the outhouse path, and in between naps dismantled as much of it as they could. Donna ripped a hole in the side and dug under it, leaving a mound of fresh dirt nearby. In August Amy tried to turn the outhouse over. She almost had it tipped on its side one day; neither she nor I realized that Vic, from Fish and Game, had wired it to the trees. Amy leaned on it with all her might and had it swinging on the wires, much to the entertainment of my guests. The trees up the hill were swaying with her every push and, at first, I thought there must be another bear up there. By the time we left for the season, the poor outhouse looked worse than it ever had. Donna and Amy's project wasn't complete, but the whole area looked worse than a plane crash when they were finished. Why did they do it? I wish I could ask them.

Taking people bear viewing by small boat is a great thing. The bears feel secure because we never get out of the boats and walk around, and the guests feel secure for the same reason. However, bears at the lodge campus are a different story. Most of the bears are just passing through, and it's fun to see them. Some of them come for people watching and to see if there is anything new going on. Bear tracking around the lodge reveals some interesting habits. The bears are well aware of the lodge schedule and know to the minute what time Mike gets up to start the generator. Often, Mike sees wet bear paw prints on the boardwalk first thing in the morning, many times on his way back up to the lodge where he had just walked minutes before. Being the second person up, sometimes I get to see them as well. Mike found James's blue towel under the porch from the year before. He hung it back up to see what would happen. In a day or so, we noticed that some bear had taken it down and "killed" it, probably in the early morning hours when they feel like they have the run of the place because we're all asleep.

The fish run at Wolverine Cove never seemed to slack off and fish were still in a huge abundance when we left in September. The bears had gotten so fat that I wondered if they could still run. The Baylee family looked like they could join the circus, they were so round. The two cubs lost the features of their little faces to fat and fur, leaving two little black shiny eyes peering out. They became the ultimate rock potatoes, entering the cove and flopping down to sleep while Baylee stuffed a few more salmon into herself. These two little bears were so stuck together I started thinking of them as the Velcro twins. That is, until I saw them get into a fur-flying fight. I think it was over a stick they were playing with. Suddenly they were tumbling and growling, biting anything and everything in their way. It was so ferocious that Baylee stopped them. She waddled up to them and grabbed a cub by the ear while pushing the other away with a paw. She cuffed them both and then rubbed noses with them. As it turned out, that was my last look at the Baylee family for the year.

The last bears I saw were Amy and Donna, who had taken to fishing together at the creek. Both of these three-year-olds had been close to the cove, but neither wanted to challenge Baylee for fishing rights. So, together they moved in. They were quite close, rubbing noses often. When I left the cove with the last guests of the year, these two were playing in the shallows together.

Next year the Velcro twins will still be with Baylee. They'll be big enough to learn how to fish and they'll spend lots of hours wrestling. Amy and Donna will be four seasons old, with personalities almost formed, learning how to be adult bears so they can be successful mothers soon.

Chapter Eight

Bears from Other Places

As we left Redoubt Bay Lodge in the fall of 2005, Mike and I decided we needed to take care of our 1927 wooden home in the Columbia Gorge before it was engulfed in blackberries and went back to the land. In 2006 we caught up with all the deferred maintenance and sold the home. This summer we are building a new home with a much smaller footprint, both physically and in terms of energy, which will be our home base. It is a comfortable walking distance to town, but we still have bears that visit in the middle of the night when the wild fruit is ripe in our little town.

Last fall we heard from Carl that he was at Redoubt Bay Lodge when the bear Amy was shot by hunters. They shot her in Wolverine Cove and then boasted that she wasn't the only one. I don't need to write how this made Carl, Amy Shapira, and everyone else who knew this bear feel. Somewhere someone has a rug of a bear they will never know.

I can't help but think of what Emmett would look like now. If he is alive he would be a mature adult bear who filled out into his lanky form to be quite majestic looking. Emmett, whose heart was bigger than most bears', is hopefully taking care of the animals around him. It saddens me to think that a hunter could take him and never know what a character Emmett was. James, if he is still alive, would have reached sexual maturity last year, and wearing his French perfume will probably be the father of many cubs. Hopefully both of these real characters will live long enough to pass on their personalities to new bears.

Mike says he can't understand why people in the lower forty-eight states have such a hard time living with bears. Many Alaskans and Canadians have been living with bears for a long time with no mortality on either side. For us, the key to living with bears was mostly in what we *didn't* do. We didn't leave food sources outside. When a bear ruined something outside, we felt it was our fault, not theirs. We didn't let bears enter buildings or hang out on the deck. We did this without hazing or averse conditioning; we simply let them know in their language where our limits were. We didn't let the teenage bears push our limits, for their own protection. I have no doubt that we could have had "pet" bears (which is what Beavis definitely wanted) but they would have been in danger of being considered "problem bears" if they were allowed to be themselves. (Cubs learn what to eat by exploring their mother's mouths with a tongue, so you can imagine getting off the plane to go bear viewing and being licked and French-kissed by a strange bear.) We didn't approach or shout at bears that we thought didn't see us. Taking our cues from the bears themselves, we tried in our own limited way to understand their needs and not deprive them of their space, food, or traditional pathways. Through knowledge of tracking and awareness of animal signs, we were able to know what the bears did when we weren't looking. This helped us to respect their space, just as we required they do for us.

The memories the bears gave me will live on for a long time. In 2002 when we first went to Redoubt Bay I had shopped for a camera, knowing I would be seeing priceless animal activity. The one I wanted cost $10,000, so I went next door to an arts and crafts store and bought fifty dollars worth of drawing materials instead. I figured that if Meriwether Lewis could teach himself to draw well enough to document his epic journey to the Pacific, so could I. That first year my drawings were primitive, but some of them had what artists call true gesture. The next seasons I tried watercolor and colored pencils, easy to use in a small cabin space in the half hour between the afternoon plane and dinner. In the fall I would redo some of these primitive paintings, and a few are framed. Last year I took a class in acrylics from a wildlife artist and now my bears are starting to come to life. I want people who look at my paintings to see the character, uniqueness, and soul of the subjects. It is a journey, just like any other, to enjoy the making of art.

I have learned to love bears, but for what they are, not what I wish they would be. I don't want to change them, influence them, or move them. Even though seeing bears is addicting, I don't have to seek them to love them. I will do what I can to influence other people to share the earth with them, and I hope you will, too.

Suggested Further Reading

Barcott, Bruce. "The Rancher and the Grizzly—A Love Story." Colorado: NRDC *OnEarth*, Winter 2007.

Craighead, Frank C., Jr. *Track of the Grizzly*. San Franciso: Sierra Club Books, 1979.

French, Steven P., MD, and Paul S. Averbach. *Management of Wilderness and Environmental Emergencies*. St. Louis: The C. V. Mosby Company, 1994.

Gunther, Kerry A., Mark A. Haroldson, Kevin Frey, Steven L. Cain, Jeff Copeland, and Charles C. Schwartz. "Grizzly Bear–Human Conflicts and Management Actions in the Greater Yellowstone Ecosystem 2001." Yellowstone National Park, Wyoming: Interagency Grizzly Bear Committee Yellowstone Ecosystem Subcommittee Report, 2001.

Herrero, Stephan. *Bear Attacks: Their Causes and Avoidance*. Guilford, Conn.: The Lyons Press, 2002.

Herrero, Stephan, Tom Smith, Terry D. DeBruyn, Kerry Gunther, and Colleen A. Matt. "From the Field: Brown Bear Habituation to People—Safety, Risks, and Benefits." *Wildlife Society Bulletin*, 2005, 33(1):362-373.

Kilham, Benjamin, and Ed Gray. *Among the Bears: Raising Orphaned Cubs in the Wild*. New York: Henry Holt Imprint, 2003.

McMillion, Scott. *Mark of the Grizzly*. Guilford, Conn.: The Lyons Press, 1998.

Lewis, M., W. Clark, and Members of the Corps of Discovery. *The Journals of the Lewis and Clark Expedition* (G. Moulton, Ed.). Lincoln: University of Nebraska Press, 2002. Retrieved Oct. 1, 2005, from the University of Nebraska Press/University of Nebraska-Lincoln Libraries-Electronic Text Center, The Journals of the Lewis and Clark Expedition Web site: http://lewisandclarkjournals.unl.edu/

Olsen, Jack. *Night of the Grizzlies*. New York: Signet, 1969.

Peacock, Doug and Andrea. *The Essential Grizzly*. Guilford, Conn: The Lyons Press, 2006.

Peterson, David. "Why I Hate (most) Hunting Magazines." Colorado: *Mountain Gazette*, 2004.

Rubbert, Tim. *Hiking with Grizzlies: Lessons Learned*. Helena, Mont.: Riverbend Publishing, 2006.

Russell, Charlie and Maureen Enns. *Grizzly Seasons: Life with the Brown Bears of Kamchatka*. Canada: Firefly Books, 2003.

Shapira, Amy and Douglas H. Chadwick. *Growing Up Grizzly: The True Story of Baylee and Her Cubs*. Helena, Mont.: Falcon Publishing, 2007.

Schullery, Paul. *Lewis and Clark among the Grizzlies: Legend and Legacy in the American West*. Helena, Mont.: Falcon Publishing, 2002.

Stringham, Stephen. *Beauty Within the Beast: Kinship With Bears in the Alaska Wilderness*. Maryland: Seven Locks Press, 2002.

Walker, Tom and Larry Aumiller. *River of Bears*. Texas: Voyageur, 1993.

Suggested Further Reading on Tracking

Elbroch, Mark. *Mammal Tracks & Sign: A Guide to North American Species.*
    Mechanicsburg, Pa: Stackpole Books, 2003

Halfpenny, James C. *A Field Guide to Mammal Tracking in North America.*
    Boulder, Colo.: Johnson Books,1986. (Available on his Web site:
    www.tracknature.com)

Hardin, Joel. *Tracker: Case Files & Adventures of a Professional Mantracker.*
    Washington: J. Hardin, 2004. (Available through his Web site:
    www.jhardin-inc.com)

Rezendes, Paul. *Tracking and the Art of Seeing: How to Read Animal
    Tracks and Sign.* 2nd ed. New York: Harper Collins, 1999.

Young, Jon and Tiffany Morgan. *Wildlife Tracking Basics.*
    Mechanicsburg, Penn: Stackpole Books, 2007.

Web Sites for Tracking

International Society of Professional Trackers
    www.ispt.org

The Bear Tracker's Den
    Kim Cabrera
    www.bear-tracker.com

Wilderness Awareness School
    Jon Young
    www.natureoutlet.com

About the Author and the Photographer

Linda Hunter worked as the lead guide and assistant manager of Redoubt Bay Lodge in Alaska for four summer seasons. She has taken thousands of people to observe brown bears in their natural habitat. As a tracker and naturalist, she has been particularly interested in studying bears since 1993. She is the cofounder of the International Society of Professional Trackers and was the first editor of *Track & Sign* newsletter. Linda has taught tracking for wilderness comfort in Washington State, has worked as a historian/naturalist on small cruise ships, and has been a licensed boat captain for thirty years. The variety of her outdoor adventures is reflected in twenty years of magazine articles about the outdoors for numerous publications. Currently, she is guiding and teaching classes from her home base in Stevenson, Washington. You can learn more about her work at www.strumminbear.com.

Amy Shapira is an award-winning bear photographer with more than ten years' experience shooting her favorite subjects in their natural habitat and is the co-author, with Douglas Chadwick of *Growing up Grizzly: The True Story of Baylee and Her Cubs* (Falcon, 2007). She has walked with black bears, has been a special visitor to the bear who starred in the movie *The Bear*, and has spent hours in all kinds of weather in Alaska watching and photographing bears. She is an active member of Vital Ground and works tirelessly for the benefit of bears worldwide, and she currently works as a volunteer at a wildlife sanctuary that rehabilitates orphaned bear cubs and releases them into the wild. Amy lives in Carbondale, Colorado.